WALKING NO



# Big Hikes in the MOURNE MOUNTAINS

by

Andrew McCluggage

KNIFE EDGE Outdoor Guidebooks

## About the Author

Andrew McCluggage is an outdoor writer and photographer from Northern Ireland. After 20 years as a corporate lawyer, he decided to do something interesting and started writing walking guidebooks.

His first book was Walking in the Briançonnais, covering a beautiful part of the French Alps. Since then, he has written a variety of guidebooks for hiking and trekking.

Other Knife Edge Outdoor Guidebooks written by Andrew include:

- **The Mourne Mountains**
- **Northern Ireland: The Unmissable Walks**
- **Trekking the Hadrian's Wall Path**
- **Trekking the South Downs Way**
- **Tour du Mont Blanc**
- **Trekking the Dolomites AV1**
- **Walker's Haute Route: Chamonix to Zermatt**
- **Trekking the Corsica GR20**
- **Walking Chamonix-Mont Blanc**
- **Walking Brittany**
- **Tour of the Écrins National Park (GR54)**

*The famous section of the Mourne Wall at Slieve Corragh*

KNIFE EDGE Outdoor Guidebooks

Publisher: Knife Edge Outdoor Limited (NI648568)
12 Torrent Business Centre, Donaghmore, County Tyrone, BT70 3BF, UK
www.knifeedgeoutdoor.com


ISBN: 978-1-912933-09-9

First edition 2021

A catalogue record for this book is available from the British Library.

**Acknowledgements:** firstly, we would like to thank Helen Cassidy for her crystal clear insights on the DRR and the Mourne 500. Without her patience, the field work for these two mammoth routes would have been a lot less pleasant! Also thank you to Rick McKee for his information on the Mourne 500 and Aaron Shimmons for his assistance with our research on the DRR.

**Front cover:** Spelga Reservoir viewed from Slieve Muck

**Title page:** The view of Carn Mountain from the summit of Doan

**This page:** Slieve Muck viewed from Pigeon Rock Mountain

All routes described in this guide have been recently walked by the author and both the author and publisher have made all reasonable efforts to ensure that all information is as accurate as possible. However, while a printed book remains constant for the life of an edition, things in the countryside often change. Trails are subject to forces outside our control. For example, landslides, tree-falls or other matters can result in damage to paths or route changes; waymarks and signposts may fade or be destroyed by wind, snow or the passage of time; or trails may not be maintained by the relevant authorities. If you notice any discrepancies between the contents of this guide and the facts on the ground, then please let us know. Our contact details are listed at the back of this book.

# Contents

*Heading towards Slieve Binnian from Carrick Little car park*

# Getting Help

## Emergency services number: dial 999

## Distress signal

The signal that you are in distress is 6 blasts on a whistle spaced over a minute, followed by a minute's silence. Then repeat. The acknowledgment that your signal has been received is 3 blasts of a whistle over a minute followed by a minute's silence. At night, flashes of a torch can also be used in the same sequences. **Always carry a torch and whistle.**

## Signalling to a helicopter from the ground

**Help Required**

Raise both arms in the shape of a 'Y'

**Help Not Required**

Raise one arm and extend the other arm down and outwards

**WARNING**

Hills, cliffs and mountains can be dangerous places and walking and running are potentially dangerous activities. Many of the routes described in this guide cross exposed and potentially hazardous terrain. You walk/run entirely at your own risk. It is solely your responsibility to ensure that you and all members of your group have adequate experience, fitness and equipment. Neither the author nor the publisher accepts any responsibility or liability whatsoever for death, injury, loss, damage or inconvenience resulting from use of this book, participation in the activity of mountain walking/running or otherwise.

Some land may be privately owned so we cannot guarantee that there is a legal right of entry to the land. Occasionally, routes change as a result of land disputes.

*The trig point on the summit of Slievemartin (Route 13)*

# Introduction

*Magnificent heather on the slopes of Slieve Binnian*

The Mournes are Northern Ireland's highest and most beautiful mountains. They form a stunning wilderness of magnificent summits and long whale-backed ridges which, in summer, are coated with bright purple heather. Uniquely, the highest peaks are completely encircled by the lovely dry-stone Mourne Wall (MW) which was completed in 1922.

In recent years, the popularity of the Mourne Mountains has soared with more hikers and runners becoming aware of their striking beauty. And this, combined with the rapid growth of long-distance hiking, endurance running and ultralight backpacking, has led to a surge of interest in challenge walks in the range. Challenge walks are tough, long-distance routes over a multitude of peaks. They normally have a theme and are longer than a normal hike/run. They are routes that push you further than you thought possible. Routes that you feel in your legs for days afterwards. Routes that you never forget.

In this book, we feature the most famous challenge walks in the Mourne Mountains and some less obvious ones too. The original Mournes challenge walk is the Mourne Wall Walk (MWW), a complete circumnavigation of the MW: see Route 1. However, more recently there has been an upswing in interest in the Seven Sevens (7-7s), a journey across the seven highest peaks in the range. Unlike the MWW, which has a relatively fixed route (defined by the course of the MW itself), the 7-7s is a more flexible affair, allowing you to choose your own route. There are clockwise and anti-clockwise routes, linear routes and circuits and a myriad of different start/finish points: everyone seems to have their own opinion on what is best. Researching the various routes is complicated so to help you decide, we describe seven different itineraries for the 7-7s: Routes 2 to 8.

We have also included two long-distance routes that we have designed: the Mournes Grand Traverse (North) and the Mournes Grand Traverse (South) are Routes 9 and 10.

These two walks are intended to showcase the Mournes by creating the most beautiful long-distance routes across the entirely of the range: they are our favourite routes, taking in all that is great about these wonderful mountains. They can be undertaken separately or be combined to form a 55km epic.

The Mourne Way (Route 11) is a long-established, but often overlooked, long-distance route around the foothills of the W and N flanks of the range. It is probably the easiest of the routes in this book and offers an entirely different perspective of the Mourne Mountains. It is extremely rewarding.

Finally, at the upper end of the difficulty scale are the Mourne 500 (Route 12) and the Denis Rankin Round (Route 13), two exceptionally challenging itineraries of 70 and 90km respectively. The Mourne 500 summits all of the points in the Mournes which are above 500m and the Denis Rankin Round scales the 39 main summits in the Mournes which are above 400m. They are extremely tough undertakings which lead you through some of the least hospitable terrain in the region but this book will help you to plan a route through these rarely-travelled places.

Tradition dictates that the challenge walks are completed in one session. But if you do not care about times or getting your name into a 'hall of fame', there is no reason why you cannot proceed more slowly, taking a few days over the routes and camping wild along the way. The MWW or the 7-7s, for example, could be hiked over two days and whilst this is not as significant a physical achievement, for many it will be a much more enjoyable one and just as rewarding. Our section on wild camping (see page 11) explains how to camp out responsibly and safely. And our section on equipment (see page 17) will help you to ensure that your pack is as light as possible.

# The Mourne Mountains

The Mourne Mountains comprise a series of beautiful heather-coated summits, each with its own personality. The highest mountain is Slieve Donard (849m), NI's highest point, which sweeps majestically down into the Irish Sea at the pretty seaside town of Newcastle. This proximity to the sea is a defining characteristic of the Mournes, often creating a mysterious atmosphere, because frequently, the high peaks can be seen rising dramatically out of a blanket of sea mist. Summiting a Mourne peak by climbing above the cloud line is an unforgettable experience.

The Mournes have everything you would expect from a mountain range on the 'Emerald Isle': beautifully long ridges, magnificent summits and vibrant heather and gorse-covered slopes. However, there is one key thing which sets them apart: uniquely, the whale-backed slopes of the highest peaks are completely encircled by the lovely dry-stone 'Mourne Wall' ('MW'). The MW was completed in 1922 and is still painstakingly maintained. It provides a stunning counterpoint to the sublime natural landscape.

The MW is 35km long (22 miles), up to 2.4m high and about 1m wide (on average). It is an amazing feat of engineering, built with locally sourced granite, which runs almost unbroken along the ridges, and over 15 of the peaks, of the Mournes. In fact, the only real gaps in this man-made structure are the few places where the wall meets cliffs and nature had already done the job.

So, what is the story of this magnificent structure? Why was it painstakingly built, stone by stone, on the top of a bunch of mountains? Well, it all had to do with water and a growing population. The problem of a reliable water supply for Belfast was first identified by the Corporation of Belfast in the 1670s. By the end of the 19th century, a growing urban population and the development of industries (such as linen and shipbuilding) had greatly exacerbated the problem. The Belfast Water Commissioners selected the valley basins of the Mourne Mountains as a solution (given the high rainfall and lack of pollution). The Commissioners promptly purchased 9,000 acres of the Mournes and commenced an ambitious schedule of infrastructure works which took many decades.

The works eventually included diverting water from the Annalong and Kilkeel rivers to a reservoir close to Belfast, constructing a dam across the Silent Valley (1923 to 1933), digging a 3.6km tunnel through Slieve Binnian to transport water from the Annalong Valley to the Silent Valley (1949 to 1952), and building a second dam to create the Ben Crom Reservoir (1954 to 1957). However, one of the earliest stages of the scheme was the construction of the MW (1904 to 1922): it was built to protect the water catchment area from interference, and pollution, by both humans and animals. The MW almost completely enclosed the Commissioners' 9,000-acre site.

The MW is still largely in pristine condition even though no mortar was used in its construction (except in the three stone shelters built on Slieve Donard, Slieve Commedagh and Slieve Meelmore). Its longevity is a testament to the hardy folk who braved all seasons to build it by hand, stone by stone.

Viewed in the 21st century, the MW is a beautiful structure in itself, built using methods and craftsmanship that are largely extinct today. As a landmark among the mountains, it somehow seems to blend in appropriately and the MW and the summits appear to have a somewhat symbiotic relationship. The MW is now so pivotal to the atmosphere of the Mournes that, without it, they would lose some of the originality and character that make them so special.

On a more practical note, the presence of the MW is comforting and reassuring for the walker/runner. On key sections of many routes, you can simply follow the wall which simplifies navigation and provides a 'security blanket' in times of low visibility. Accordingly, it is understandable that those who know the Mournes well view the MW with a mixture of respect and affection.

If you want to explore the Mournes further, there is a sister volume to this book which should help: it is entitled 'The Mourne Mountains' and includes 30 of the best walks in the range (see the inside back cover).

## Game of Thrones locations

It is widely known that NI served as a stunning backdrop for many of the finest scenes in Game of Thrones, the incredibly addictive television series. But working out exactly where the locations are can be quite tricky. The following three Mourne Mountain places were used as Game of Thrones locations:

- **Sandy Brae near Attical:** in season one, the countryside here was used as the entrance to Vaes Dothrak. Route 12 uses Sandy Brae, which starts as a small road and becomes a rough track.
- **Tollymore Forest Park:** apparently, this was the location for the Haunted Forest where the white walkers began their march into the realms of men. If you want to try to spot a dire-wolf, then try Route 11 which takes in most of the forest's highlights.
- **Leitrim Lodge:** the hills in this area provided the landscape for Bran Stark's flight north of Winterfell. Routes 10 to 13 all visit this area

# When to hike/run

Usually, you can walk/run in the Mournes at any time of year and each season has plenty to commend it. Even in winter, there is rarely snow in sufficient quantities to prevent normal hill-walking. However, long-distance routes are more serious physical challenges and are therefore best saved for the drier months: you will travel more quickly over hard, dry ground and expend less energy. Normally, conditions are driest between late April and late September.

You should also give consideration to the number of hours of daylight that you will need to complete your challenge. It is much more difficult hiking/running in darkness and the chance of injury is greater. The longest day of the year is 21 June (the summer solstice): days are progressively shorter either side of that date.

Those undertaking the DRR (which travels the rough terrain to the far W of the range) should also bear in mind that the grass grows longer as the summer progresses, making hiking and running these areas more difficult.

**Spring** (March to May): this can be the most beautiful time of year. Many wild-flowers are on show including daffodils, rhododendrons and primroses. The gorse will also be in full bloom with its vivid yellow flowers and coconut aroma. By May, new growth will be upon the larches and other deciduous plants and the weather is often sunny and warm. Indeed, May can be the finest month in Ireland. Visibility in spring is generally excellent so views are wide-ranging. Of course, rain is still a possibility at this time of year but it usually becomes less likely as the season progresses.

**Summer** (June to August): this is the peak walking season and there are a high number of walkers and runners. Temperatures are at their peak, however, there is sometimes haze. Summer also sees the heather in full bloom, covering the mountains with a beautiful purple carpet.

**Autumn** (September to November): holidaymakers are generally back at work and schools have started so the Mournes are quieter, particularly mid-week. Autumn sometimes provides the best walking/running conditions. The weather in September and October can be quite settled, with less rain than in summer. Temperatures are lower but still comfortable. Skies can be very clear giving excellent visibility and the quality of the low light is magnificent. The wide variety of deciduous plants in NI means that the autumn colours are stunning. However, as the days get shorter, it is wise to start walking early. If something were to go wrong, you would have less daylight in which to seek help than in summer.

**Winter** (December to February): these are the coldest months and although snow can fall on the high peaks, heavy snow is not that common these days. A light sprinkling of snow in the Mournes can be a delight for a suitably equipped walker although care should be taken. However, walking in deep snow is best left to those with the appropriate winter mountain experience and the correct equipment. Even if there is no snow, watch out for ice which forms in the many places where water collects. Cold months often bring crisp, clear weather and the low sun makes the light very beautiful. A sunny day in winter can be one of the best of the year. Days are short so start early.

| Season | Pros | Cons |
|---|---|---|
| Spring | Pleasant temperatures<br>Frequent sunny skies<br>Good visibility<br>Gorse and wild-flowers<br>Fewer visitors | Rainy spells are common in March and April<br>Ground can be wet |
| Summer | Generally reliably fine weather<br>Heather season | Sometimes hazy<br>Visitor numbers highest |
| Autumn | Pleasant temperatures<br>Frequent sunny skies<br>Excellent visibility<br>Fewer visitors<br>Autumn colours | Shorter days<br>Cooler evenings<br>Rainy spells |
| Winter | Sometimes crisp clear skies<br>Excellent visibility<br>Fewer visitors | Shortest days<br>Can be cold and icy<br>Occasionally, there is snow |

*Slieve Beurnagh*

# Preparation

All of the routes in this book are significant undertakings and are not suitable for beginners. You should not attempt them without adequate preparation: this is true for both hikers and runners.

**Physical preparation:** detailed advice on fitness training is beyond the scope of this book but, in simple terms, you should ensure that you are fit enough to complete the route you are attempting. If you find mid-route that you are unable to continue, you put yourself, your companions and members of any rescue team at risk.

The best way to gauge fitness for a challenge route is to complete a series of training hikes/runs. Start off with shorter routes and work up towards the distance/altitude gain of the challenge you wish to attempt. For example, if attempting the 7-7s, your training could involve a series of progressively longer routes until you can successfully complete four or five of the summits in one session: at that point, you are likely to be ready to attempt the full seven peaks. Training hikes will also help you to accurately estimate the time you need to complete the challenge and increase the likelihood that you will get your pacing right during your attempt. The sister volume to this book, 'The Mourne Mountains', contains 30 different routes of different lengths and many of these would be suitable training hikes.

**Navigation skills:** the routes in this book take place in the high mountains. Weather conditions can change rapidly and, although you may be confident navigating in clear conditions, route finding in low visibility is much more difficult. To keep yourself and your companions safe, you should always carry a map and compass and you should know how to use them. If you do not know how to navigate with a map and compass then it is wise to attend a navigation course. Even if you are not a novice, it could pay to brush up on your navigation skills before your attempt.

**Route planning:** decide well in advance what route you are going to take and estimate how much time you will need. Learn the route off by heart so that you can follow it on a map without hesitation. It is a good idea to reconnoitre the difficult parts of the route in advance so that you know what to expect on the day of your attempt: you can carry out your reconnaissance on training hikes. This is particularly true of parts of the Mourne 500 and the DRR which lead you through some difficult terrain, with no paths, where navigation (even in clear conditions) requires care. If you make a navigational error on these routes then you may have to back-track significantly and the additional time and distance could result in failure. As part of your route planning exercise, identify possible escape routes in case something goes wrong (see 'Escape routes').

**Equipment preparation:** ensure that you have all the equipment you require well in advance of your attempt. It is a good idea to have tested your gear on training hikes/runs so that you are familiar with it. You want to be sure that the backpack, clothes and shoes you will use are comfortable and effective. For advice on equipment, see page 17.

# Using this book

**Timings** for long-distance routes are difficult to estimate accurately in a book such as this one. This is because every runner/hiker travels at very different speeds. Some of the best runners, for example, can complete the 7-7s in 3.5hr or less. Some hikers on the other hand may require 12hr or more to finish. For this reason, we give suggested timings for each route as a broad range: the ranges only provide rough guidance and you will need to work out where you fall within the range. Once you have completed a few training hikes/runs then you will have a better idea of your timings. The Mourne 500 and the DRR are so long that estimates of timings are practically useless.

**Walking distances** are given in both miles and kilometres (km) but road distances are given in miles only. This is because road signs in the UK use miles but NI mapping grids use kilometres. One mile equates to approximately 1.6km.

**Place names in brackets** indicate the direction to be followed on signposts. For example, "('Newcastle')" would mean that you follow a sign for Newcastle.

**Ascent data** for a route is the aggregate altitude gain over the entire route: the total metres/feet that you will climb. As a rule of thumb, a fit walker climbs 300 to 400m (1000 to 1300ft) in an hour.

**Elevation profiles** are provided for each route. These profiles tell you where the climbs and descents fall on the route.

**Two types of maps** are provided. Firstly, for each route, there is a small-scale topographical map on which the route has been marked. These maps are for planning purposes so that you can understand the overall extent of the routes. Secondly, at the back of the book, there are extracts from OSNI's Activity Map: the Mournes (1:25,000). These maps cover the entire geographical area used by this book and are designed to enable you to study the routes more closely. To enable you to use the OSNI maps for navigation, we have tried, as far as possible, to keep them free of clutter. Accordingly, we have not marked route lines on them: instead, we have added a series of coloured waypoints which link to the written directions provided for each route. Because the routes are so long, they often share waypoints. The colour coding of the waypoints works as follows:

- **MWW (Route 1):** red waypoints only
- **7-7s (Routes 2 to 8):** some red waypoints (that are shared with the MWW) plus some new blue waypoints
- **MGTN/MGTS (Routes 9 & 10):** red and blue waypoints that are shared with the MWW/7-7s plus some new yellow waypoints
- **The Mourne Way (Route 11):** orange waypoints plus a few yellow waypoints that are shared with the MGTN
- **Mourne 500 (Route 12):** this is a huge route so there is a combination of yellow, blue and red waypoints plus some new green ones
- **DRR (Route 13):** the longest route which uses green, orange, yellow, blue, and red waypoints plus some new purple ones

**Grid references** are occasionally provided in the walk descriptions: 'IG' stands for 'Irish Grid'.

**Spellings of place names** are normally derived from the OSNI maps. However, there is sometimes disagreement over how places are spelt. Accordingly, you may notice different spellings elsewhere.

## The following abbreviations are used:

| | |
|---|---|
| 7-7s | The Seven Sevens |
| DRR | Denis Rankin Round |
| MGTN | Mournes Grand Traverse (North) |
| MGTS | Mournes Grand Traverse (South) |
| MW | Mourne Wall |
| MWW | Mourne Wall Walk |
| NI | Northern Ireland |
| OSNI | Ordnance Survey Northern Ireland |
| TL | Turn left |
| TR | Turn right |
| SH | Straight ahead |
| N, S, E and W, etc. | North, South, East and West, etc. |

**Exact locations of start points** are provided for each walk. To make life easier, we have used the global addressing system devised by what3words. It is one of the simplest ways to talk about location and is much easier to use than traditional coordinate systems. what3words has divided the world into 3mx3m squares, each with a unique 3-word address. You can download the what3words smartphone app (free of charge) from your app store. If you type one of the 3-word addresses into the search box in the app, it will display the location and provide directions to it.

*Cock Mountain seen from the summit of Tornamrock*

# Wild Camping

In NI there is no 'right to roam'. The land in the Mourne Mountains is privately owned and we are permitted to walk there with the generous permission of the landowners. Technically therefore, you require the consent of the relevant landowner to camp out. However, although it has not (to our knowledge) expressly been sanctioned, wild camping has long been tolerated in the Mournes. With the increased popularity of the region, the number of wild campers has grown in recent years. It is therefore more important than ever to respect the land and the landowners' wishes. All those enjoying the priceless privilege of spending the night in these wonderful mountains should follow some important rules:

- **Leave no trace:** you should leave the environment in exactly the same condition as you found it. Take away all rubbish and leave nothing behind. When you have packed up and are ready to leave, look back on your campsite and make sure that another person would not be able to tell that you have been there (except for the flattened grass where your tent was pitched).
- **Never light an open fire:** climate change is upon us and bush-fires are becoming more common. At the time of writing, one of the worst bush-fires in the Mournes in living memory had just destroyed vast parts of the slopes of Slieve Donard. In our opinion, open fires and portable barbecues simply carry too much risk. Do not be that person who accidentally destroys acres of the Mournes.
- **Perform toilet duties responsibly:** this means that you should use a trowel to dig a hole in which you 'do your business'. There are some incredibly lightweight backpacking trowels available these days. Your hole should be at least 30m from water-courses. Fill the hole in afterwards and take home your used toilet paper in a bag that you have brought along specifically for that purpose. Defecating and placing a stone on top is not acceptable: imagine how you would feel if you sat down next to that stone! Also carry out tampons and sanitary towels.
- **Be discreet and have respect for others:** try to camp where others cannot see you. Keep your group small: it is supposed to be a 'wild' experience. Do not make a lot of noise at night.
- **Stay only one night at each spot**

The obvious downside to wild camping is that you need to carry a lot more gear: tents, sleeping mats, sleeping bags and stoves all add weight to your pack, making the routes more difficult. In the 'Equipment' section, we provide advice on how to lighten your load.

**For your own safety, do not camp wild during very dry periods when there is a higher risk of bushfire.**

*Heading towards Spelga Mountain on the Mourne Way (Route 11)*

# On the Trail

*One of the many stiles over the MW*

## Weather

The island of Ireland is known as the 'Emerald Isle' for good reason and its beautiful greenery requires plenty of water. This water is of course supplied by rain and Ireland's location right on the edge of the Atlantic Ocean ensures that there is plenty of it: the island bears the brunt of many Atlantic fronts as they make their way eastwards.

In the Mourne Mountains, conditions can change rapidly and Mourne Mountain Rescue Team get plenty of 'business' each year from those who get caught out. It is prudent therefore for the walker to be prepared for rain and low visibility. Mountains can be dangerous places and need to be treated with respect and caution even if the weather forecast is favourable.

Always get a weather forecast before setting out. Many internet sites provide forecasts, with a varying degree of reliability. The UK Met Office (www.metoffice.gov.uk) is one of the most reliable as it provides regularly updated localised forecasts for different places in NI. It also provides, free of charge, an excellent smartphone app that gives local forecasts.

## Maps

The best sheet maps for walking in the Mournes are OSNI's Activity Map: the Mournes (1:25,000) and Harvey's Mourne Mountains Superwalker XT25 (1:25,000). Extracts from the OSNI map are set out at the back of this book. Altitudes and place names referred to in this book are derived, where possible, from the OSNI maps: occasionally, altitudes and names on Harvey's map differ slightly from those on the OSNI map.

## Terrain and navigation

All of the routes in this book are long and challenging and cross exposed and potentially hazardous terrain: a fall could have serious consequences. In the Mournes, do not assume that your entire route will use clearly defined paths and tracks. Although there are good paths on the most popular sections, particularly in the E of the range, in other places there are long sections without paths over grass, heather or peat bog. Often the ground is wet underfoot.

Although waymarks are rare, in good conditions, route-finding is largely straightforward in areas where dry-stone walls (such as the MW) assist with navigation. However, in other places, particularly in the W of the range, navigation can be more tricky even in good conditions. In low visibility or bad weather, the Mournes can be a confusing place so always carry a map and compass and know how to use them.

## Accessing start/finish points

There is car parking at all the start and finish points used in this book. However, with the recent surge in popularity of the Mournes, it can sometimes be difficult to get a space, particularly at weekends and during school holidays: the earlier you arrive the better. For linear walks, you could park a car at both ends of the route. However, a popular alternative is to use the **Mourne Shuttle Service** (07516 412076; advance booking essential): park at your finish point and the shuttle will transport you from there to the start point.

Alternatively, from May to August, Translink usually runs the **Mourne Rambler** service. This is a hop on/hop off bus which runs in a loop through the Mournes, starting and finishing at Newcastle bus station and passing near most of the walk start/finish points. Occasionally, the bus stops are a short walk away from the exact starting point. It usually runs five times a day (excluding Mondays) in an anti-clockwise direction, stopping at:

- Tollymore Forest Park
- Trassey Road: Trassey Track is ¾mile from the stop
- Moyad Road: Happy Valley car park is ½mile from the stop
- Ott Mountain car park
- Spelga Dam
- Banns Road car park
- Attical
- Silent Valley
- Carrick Little car park
- Rourkes Park
- Bloody Bridge

Using the service, you could catch an early bus from Newcastle to the start point of your chosen route and then catch a later bus back to Newcastle when you have finished. For further information, see www.translink.co.uk or call Newcastle Visitor Information Centre (028 4372 2222).

As an alternative, a number of local taxi businesses operate transport services: Shimna Taxis (028 4372 3030) or Donard Cabs (028 4372 4100).

# Drinking water

On long-distance routes, drinking water should be one of your primary considerations. Even in NI, the sun can be hot: dehydration and sunstroke are always possibilities. Water is heavy and therefore it is not always possible to start a long-distance route carrying all that you will need. Finding water on the trail can be tricky so it requires careful planning. In the introduction to each route, we list some of the places (rivers, streams and lakes) where water is normally available, however, often there are other smaller streams along the way which can also be useful. We have also marked key water points on the OSNI maps at the back of this book using the following icon: . Bear in mind that availability of water in streams may vary depending upon the season and the amount of rainfall over previous weeks and months. There are also two springs which hikers/runners frequently use (look out for small pipes from which running water flows):

- **Slieve Meelmore spring**: close to the W side of the MW, SE of 13
- **Slieve Commedagh spring**: close to the S side of the MW, W of 17

It can be a good idea to prepare a written 'water plan'. Taking into account the weather on the day of your attempt, estimate how much water you will need to cover the entire route (your total consumption): if you have completed training hikes then you should have a reasonable idea. Remember that on hot days you will need more water than on cooler ones. Then work out where the possible water points are on the route and identify which ones you will need to use. Now divide your total consumption up across the route, estimating how much water you will need between each water point that you have selected. Always be clear about where your next water point will be and always check your water levels when you pass a water point. Furthermore, it is good practice to ensure that when you leave a water point, you have 0.5l of surplus water (in case your estimates prove to be inaccurate or your next water point is dry).

Although some do it, we would never recommend drinking water from a spring, river, stream or lake without first dealing with possible contaminants including visible particulates (which sometimes give stream water a brown colour), bacteria, viruses, protozoa (for example, giardia) and parasites. There are a variety of possible ways to treat water.

- **Boiling** is the traditional method. A rolling boil of 1min should kill everything in the water. However, it does not remove visible particulates so the boiled water will remain the same colour as when you found it, which can be off-putting. It also uses up a lot of fuel and takes time so is impractical if you are moving quickly.
- **Filtering** usually removes visible particulates, working miracles by turning coloured water clear. Normally, it also removes 99.9% of bacteria, protozoa and parasites. Filters are often cheap and light. It is the quickest method of treatment so it is useful for long-distance routes. However, most filters cannot remove viruses so, if you are concerned about them, you will need to combine filtering with another method such as boiling, UV or chemical treatment.
- **Chemical treatment** can remove bacteria, protozoa, viruses and parasites but each product is different so read the labels carefully. However, there are many disadvantages to chemicals: it does not remove visible particulates so the water will remain the same colour as when you found it; water treated with chemicals usually has a taste; the water usually cannot be drunk immediately as chemicals take time to kill pathogens; and from a health perspective, consuming chemicals may not be good for you.

- **UV treatment** kills bacteria, protozoa, viruses and parasites. However, it does not remove visible particulates so the water will remain the same colour as when you found it: coloured water can be off-putting and the UV treatment is less effective if the water is not completely clear. The most common products are Steripens which are very light.

| | Visible Particulates | Bacteria | Virus | Protozoa | Parasites |
|---|---|---|---|---|---|
| **Boiling** | ✗ | ✓ | ✓ | ✓ | ✓ |
| **Filter** | ✓ | ✓ | ✗ | ✓ | ✓ |
| **Chemical Treatment** | ✗ | ✓ | ✓ | ✓ | ✓ |
| **UV Treatment (such as Steripen)** | ✗ | ✓ | ✓ | ✓ | ✓ |

Perhaps the best single method for the Mournes is filtering as the water there is frequently coloured. Filtering turns it clear and removes almost everything except viruses: although it is possible, you are unlikely to encounter virus in Mourne water and some are prepared to drink water which has only been filtered, running a small risk of virus contamination. However, we prefer to combine filtration with UV treatment (using a Steripen): this removes or kills practically everything.

The actual effectiveness of individual products varies and is beyond the scope of this book so do your research beforehand. However, it is worth noting that many products claim to be 99.9% effective indicating that drinking water from wild sources can never be said to be 100% risk free. You will have to weigh up the risks and make up your own mind. You drink the water at your own risk!

If, like many, you do decide to drink the water in the Mournes then, as well as treating the water, there are a few rules that you should follow to reduce further any risk:

- Avoid water where there is evidence nearby of animals, especially cows or sheep: carcasses (of dead animals) or faeces can cause contamination
- Do not collect water downstream from buildings or grazing areas
- Preferably drink from moving water. The faster the better
- The bigger the river/stream the better
- Generally the higher the altitude the better

## Escape routes

On each hike, there are a number of 'escape routes': places from which you can head directly to a road, village or town. These are useful if something goes wrong, you need to seek help or weather conditions deteriorate. Before you start your attempt, it is advisable to have a clear understanding of where the relevant escape routes are. We list a selection of escape routes in the introduction to each hike but there are many other possible ways of getting off the mountains.

# Equipment

*The MW crossing the summit of Slieve Loughshannagh*

When undertaking any route in the mountains, you should be properly equipped for the worst terrain and the worst weather conditions which you could encounter. In the Mournes, rain is a key consideration in all seasons: you might not get any in practice but you should expect it when planning and ensure that you carry waterproofs. You should also be equipped for cold conditions even in summer: getting cold and/or wet in the hills is unpleasant and can be dangerous. In late spring, summer and early autumn, you should also carry gear that protects you from the sun. However, the dilemma is that you should also consider weight and avoid carrying anything unnecessary. The heavier your pack, the more energy you will expend.

## Recommended basic kit

Layering of clothing is the key to warmth: warm air gets trapped between the layers, acting as insulation. Merino wool or man-made materials are preferable: they wick moisture away from the skin, keeping you warm. Do not wear cotton: it does not dry quickly and gets cold.

| | | |
|---|---|---|
| **Boots/Shoes** | Good quality, properly fitting and worn in. Some like trail-running shoes but others prefer boots with ankle support. | |
| **Gaiters** | Useful in areas where the ground is wet and boggy. | |
| **Socks** | Good quality, quick drying walking/running socks. | |
| **Waterproof jacket and trousers** | Waterproof and breathable. Some people do not bother with waterproof trousers but we like to carry light ones just in case. | |
| **Base layer** | T-shirts and underwear of man-made fabrics/merino wool which wick moisture away from your body. | |
| **Fleece** | It can be cold even in summer. Man-made fabrics. | |

| | |
|---|---|
| **Shorts/ Trousers** | For hikers, light walking trousers are normally adequate in spring and summer. Convertible ones are practical as you can remove the legs on warm days. In autumn and winter, you may need something warmer. |
| **Warm hat and gloves** | Even in summer it can be cold, especially in the evening and early morning. |
| **Rucksack** | 30-35 litres is adequate for day-hikers. 40-50 litres should be sufficient for campers. Well-padded shoulder straps and waist band are important. Much of the weight of the pack should rest on your hips rather than your shoulders. |
| **Waterproof pack liner** | Rucksacks are not very waterproof. A liner will keep your gear dry if it rains. |
| **Whistle** | For emergencies. Many rucksacks have one incorporated into the sternum strap. |
| **Head-torch with spare batteries** | It is good practice to carry a head-torch for emergencies. This can help you if you get caught out late and enables you to signal to rescuers. |
| **Basic first-aid kit** | Including plasters, a bandage and antiseptic wipes. |
| **Map and compass** | For maps see above. A GPS unit or a smartphone app can be a useful addition but they are no substitute for a map and compass: after all, batteries can run out and electronics can fail. |
| **Sunglasses, sun-hat, sunscreen and lip-salve** | Even in NI, the sun can be strong so do not set out without these items. |
| **Walking poles** | These transfer weight from your legs onto your arms, keeping you fresher. They also save your knees (particularly on descents) and can reduce the likelihood of falling or twisting an ankle. |
| **Phone** | A smartphone is a very useful tool. It can be used for emergencies. Furthermore, apps for weather and mapping are invaluable. It can also replace your camera to save weight. |
| **Space blanket or emergency bag** | Very light and it could save your life. |
| **Food** | Carry some emergency food. Energy bars, nuts and dried fruit are all good. |
| **Water** | Start with at least 1.5 litres of water per person. Hydration packs with tubes facilitate more effective hydration by enabling drinking on the move. |

# Ultralight gear for wild campers

A hiker has no influence over challenges like weather and terrain but can control the contents of a pack carried on the trail. Obviously, those intending to wild camp will need to carry more gear than day-hikers. It is even more important therefore for campers to focus on choice of equipment. The lighter your pack, the less energy you expend, the faster you can move and the more you will enjoy your trip.

A hiker's base-weight is the weight of his/her pack, excluding food and water. Some campers struggle over the summits of the Mournes with a base-weight of 15kg or more. However, by investing in some modern lightweight gear, it is possible for campers to achieve a base-weight of 6-7kg or less. The differences in the weights of different products are surprisingly large so it pays to do some thorough research before buying. Many people are quick to tell you that the lighter the gear, the greater the price but that is not always the case. While it is true that lightweight gear can be expensive, there are also some excellent lightweight products which are great value. Tents, sleeping bags and backpacks are the three heaviest items that you will carry so they offer the biggest opportunities for weight-saving. But do not ignore the smaller items either as the weight can quickly add up. Be ruthless as every ounce counts.

**Tent:** this is one of the heaviest things that you will carry so It provides a big opportunity for weight saving. Some 2-person tents weigh more than 3kg while others weigh less than 0.6kg. The heaviest ones are normally built for extreme winter conditions and are overkill for the summer. However, the lightest ones are less durable. Although a few premium brands charge a lot for their products and there are some very expensive tents at the lightest end of the scale, these days there are plenty of lightweight tents available at a reasonable price. Tents weighing 1 to 1.5kg often strike a good balance between price, longevity and weight.

Your tent should be waterproof to ensure that you stay dry during rainy nights. If you are going to use a very light tent then a footprint can be a good idea to protect its base: 'footprint' is a trendy, modern word for what used to be known as a groundsheet. Sometimes you can buy footprints specific to your tent model but we prefer to use a sheet of Tyvek which can be cut to size: Tyvek is extremely tough and is cheaper, and normally lighter, than most branded footprints.

**Tent Pegs:** tent weights provided by manufacturers normally exclude the weight of the pegs. The pegs actually provided with tents tend to be quite heavy and many trekkers buy replacement ones which are lighter. Six heavy pegs can weigh as much as 240g while 6 light pegs can weigh as little as 6g. Titanium pegs offer a good balance between weight and strength. There are many different types available these days and it is important to match the peg with the type of ground they will be used in. The ground in the Mournes is normally soft and grassy so it is usually easy to get pegs into it. Accordingly, they do not need to be too strong and heavy.

**Sleeping bag:** each bag has a 'comfort rating': This is the lowest temperature at which the standard woman should enjoy a comfortable night's sleep. There is also a 'lower comfort limit' which is for men. That may sound simple but it is not. Although all reputable sleeping bag manufacturers use the same independent standard, the bags are not tested in the same place so there is a lack of consistency amongst ratings. Also, the ratings are designed with an average man and woman in mind but every person is different: some people get colder than others. The ratings should therefore be used as a guide only and it is wise to choose a bag with a comfort rating which is a few degrees lower than the night temperatures that you will encounter. In June, July and August a bag rated between 5 and

10°C is normally sufficient, depending on whether you 'sleep hot' or 'sleep cold'. In early and late season, you may want something warmer. However, you do not want to bring a bag that is much too warm as that would add unnecessary weight to your pack.

Unfortunately, with sleeping bags, price tends to be inversely proportional to weight. This is largely because the lightest bags are filled with goose/duck down which is expensive. Synthetic bags are also available but they are much heavier so down is the better choice. The disadvantage of down bags is that they can lose their warmth if they get wet but that is less likely if you have a good tent and pack liner. Our advice is first to decide what comfort rating you will require. Then choose the lightest bag (with that rating) which you can afford.

**Sleeping mat:** this serves two purposes. Firstly, it makes it comfortable for you to sleep on the hard ground. Secondly, it insulates you from the ground's cold surface. There are three types: air, self-inflating and closed-cell foam. The advantages and disadvantages of each are set out below. Unless you are camping out in very cold conditions, weight is normally more of an issue than warmth so we prefer air mats.

| Sleeping Mat Type | Pros | Cons |
|---|---|---|
| **Air mats:** need to be blown up | Lightest<br>Very comfortable<br>Most compact when packed<br>Thicker: good for side sleepers | Most expensive<br>Hard work to inflate<br>Can be punctured<br>Less warm than self-inflating |
| **Self-inflating mats:** a combination of air and closed-cell foam. The mat partially inflates itself when the valve is opened | Warmest<br>Very comfortable<br>Quite compact<br>More durable than air mats<br>Firmness is adjustable by adding air | Heavier<br>More expensive than closed-cell foam<br>Can be punctured |
| **Closed-cell foam mats** | Light<br>Least expensive<br>Most durable<br>Cannot be punctured | Not compact: need to be strapped to the outside of your pack<br>Least warm<br>Least comfortable |

**Pillow:** some use rolled-up clothing but we prefer inflatable trekking pillows which only weigh around 50g.

**Stove:** it is sensible to choose a stove that uses a type of fuel which is widely available. Multi-fuel stoves that burn petrol are useful as you can obtain fuel at any service station. And both gas and methylated spirits are stocked in outdoor shops in NI. Gas is the cleanest fuel to use and is the most popular. Most gas stoves are designed to fit generic screw-on canisters (not Campinggaz) which are readily available in NI. Canisters for Campinggaz stoves (which are popular in France) are much harder to find so are not a good choice in NI.

Hundreds of different stoves are available, some more complicated than others. Often the lightest ones are the most simple and often the most simple ones are relatively inexpensive. If, like most campers, you will eat dried food such as pasta and rice then your stove will need to do little more than boil water. A basic stove which mounts on top of a gas canister will therefore be adequate: such a stove should also be cheap and lightweight (less than 100g).

**Pots:** if, like most campers, you eat dried food such as pasta and rice then you will only need one pot which will do little more than boil water. To save weight, go for the smallest pot that you can get away with. For example, if you are travelling solo and planning to use freeze-dried backpacking meals then you would need nothing bigger than a 500-600ml pot. Titanium pots are usually the lightest but they are slightly more expensive. Get the lightest one that you can afford.

**Fork/Spoon:** we love Sporks! They have a spoon at one end and a fork at the other. They weigh a mere 9g and cost very little.

*Slievemoughanmore viewed from the summit of Wee Slievemoughan*

# Safety

Spelga Reservoir

On a calm summer day, the mountains are paradise but a sudden weather shift or an injury can change things dramatically. Treat the environment with respect and be conscious of your experience levels and physical capabilities. The following is a non-exhaustive list of recommendations:

- The fitter you are, the more you will enjoy your challenge.
- Before you set out, study the route and make plans based upon the abilities of the weakest member of your party.
- Get a weather forecast and reassess your plans in light of it. Avoid exposed routes if the weather is uncertain.
- Start early to avoid ascending during the hottest part of the day and to allow more surplus time in case something goes wrong.
- Do not stray from the route so as to avoid getting lost and to help prevent erosion of the landscape.
- Never be too proud to turn back if you find the going too tough or if the weather deteriorates.
- Bring a map and compass and know how to use them.
- It is sensible to tell someone where you are going and when you expect to return. If you do not return then they can raise the alarm.
- Carry surplus food and clothing for emergencies.
- In the event of an accident, move an injured person to a safe place and administer any necessary first-aid. Keep the victim warm. Establish your exact coordinates and, if possible, use your mobile phone to call for help. The emergency number is 999. If you have no signal then send someone for help.
- Avoid exposed high ground in a thunderstorm. If you get caught out in one then drop your walking poles and stay away from trees, overhanging rocks, metal structures and caves. Generally accepted advice is to squat on your pack and keep as low as possible.
- Do not scramble with walking poles in your hands. Stow them away before you start to scramble to keep your hands free. The number of hikers who clamber up exposed rocks with poles in their hands is staggering: this is very dangerous.

# General Information

*Many of the routes start/finish in Newcastle*

**Language:** English is the main language.

**Charging electronic devices:** the UK uses a 3 pin plug

**Money:** NI uses Sterling. ATMs can be found in most towns and in many service stations but rarely in smaller villages. Credit cards are accepted almost everywhere.

**Visas:** NI is part of the UK. Currently, citizens of the EU, Australia, New Zealand, Canada and the US do not need a visa for short tourist trips to Ireland or the UK.

**Mobile phones:** there is network in most towns and villages. In the mountains, however, it can sometimes be difficult to get a signal.

**International dialling codes:** the country code for the UK is +44. For the Republic of Ireland it is +353. In both cases, you omit the first 0 in the area code if dialling from overseas.

**WiFi:** nearly all hotels and B&Bs have wifi.

**Insurance:** it is wise for visitors from outside the UK to have adequate travel insurance which covers hiking.

**Emergencies and mountain rescue:** Mourne Mountain Rescue Team is a charity financed by grants and public donations. Their services are free and are provided by unpaid volunteers. The emergency number is 999: ask for 'mountain rescue'.

**Ticks:** as is often the case in Europe, ticks are present in NI. They can carry Lyme disease or tick-borne encephalitis so check yourself regularly. Remove ticks with a tick removal tool (making sure that you get all of it out) and then disinfect the area.

**Tourist information:** tourist information for NI is available at one of the many Visitor Information Centres. Information (including contact details for the Visitor Information Centres) can also be found at www.discovernorthernireland.com.

*Slieve Commedagh viewed from the summit of Slieve Donard*

# Wildlife & Plants

**Wildlife:** the fauna in NI is similar to that in other parts of Ireland or the UK. There are deer, foxes, badgers, rabbits, squirrels, hedgehogs, mice and shrews. There are also hares but these are relatively rare nowadays. Tollymore Forest Park has one of the largest colonies of red squirrels on the island of Ireland. Otters are present in some rivers although they are rare. In the high Mournes, mammals (other than sheep) are few and far between: you are much more likely to spot an animal in the surrounding hedgerows and forests.

Much of the bird life is also similar to that in other parts of Ireland or the UK. Magpies and crows are ubiquitous as are many of the usual species of small birds. Thankfully, buzzards are now common again after a difficult 20th century. Jays, ravens, woodpeckers, pheasants and grouse can also be seen. However, it is near the coast where you tend to spot the most interesting birds: fulmars, gannets, guillemots, kittiwakes, oyster-catchers, terns, curlews, herons and cormorants.

The nearby Strangford Lough is one of the finest bird sanctuaries in Europe. As well as many other species, 95% of the world's population of Canadian light-bellied brent geese are thought to be present there in autumn. Strangford Lough also has more than 2000 marine species and 28 of those are found nowhere else in the world.

**Plants:** much of the countryside in NI is arable or pastoral farmland. There are forests too and common trees include ash, beech, birch and oak. Larch trees are also common but sadly, the emergence of Japanese larch disease has resulted in the felling of large sections of larch forest. Evidence of this devastation can be seen from the Trassey Track.

One of the most widespread plants in NI is gorse (known locally as 'whins') and its yellow flowers are a dominating feature of the countryside in spring. Anyone who walks through a section of bright gorse (pictured above) will be struck by the mouth-watering coconut aroma.

In the hills and mountains of NI, the peaty soil is generally less fertile so there is a smaller range of plants. Heather is everywhere and when it flowers in summer, the hills take on a gorgeous purple hue. Sphagnum moss with its pink or green colours is found wherever it is very damp, as is bog myrtle, bog asphodel and bog cotton: the latter is easily spotted in summer with its fluffy white head. The colourful rhododendron, an imposter, is common around the fringes of the mountains but not in the vast quantities which plague the indigenous plants in the west of Ireland.

*The Mourne Way heading towards Hen Mountain (Route 11)*

# Route Descriptions

# 1 The Mourne Wall Walk

This is the original challenge walk in the Mournes and is arguably the longest and finest ridge walk in all of Ireland. It is also one of the hardest. The route involves almost a complete circumnavigation of the magnificent MW, climbing 15 named peaks on the way, including six of the seven highest mountains in the range. From the summit of Slieve Muck, you remain on the main Mourne ridge for an unbelievable 17km and the views are exquisite.

However, the terrain is relentless, alternately climbing and descending throughout. Most fit hikers can complete the walk in one long summer day and runners do it much more quickly. However, it is lovely to spend two days doing it, wild camping somewhere along the way. An overnight beside the MW is a wonderful experience.

In the 1950s, the Youth Hostel Association of Northern Ireland first organised an annual Mourne Wall Walk. Participation steadily grew over the years and by the late 1970s more than 3,000 people were signing up for the event each year. Environmentalists began to raise concerns that the Mournes were being damaged by the sheer volume of people hiking on a single day. In 1984, the event was cancelled and it has not taken place since.

As the route has long, exposed sections, it is best saved for a fine day. Navigation is normally straightforward as mostly you follow the MW. However, finding safe passage between Slieve Binnian and Wee Binnian can be difficult. In this area, there are many cliffs and steep crags, which you must avoid.

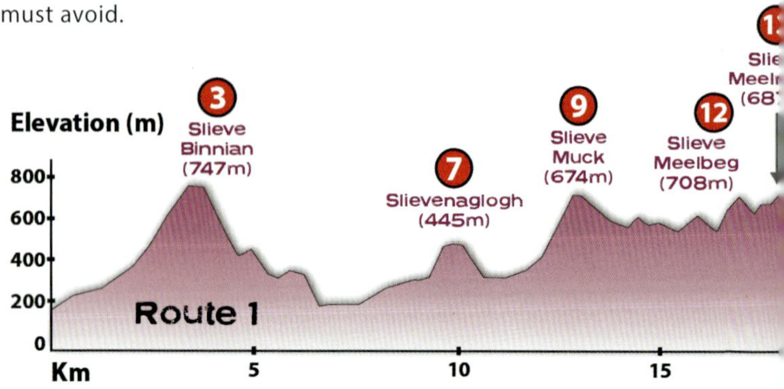

*One of the many stiles over the MW*

| | |
|---|---|
| Time (hr) | 5 to 13 |
| Distance | 33.4km/20.8 miles |
| Total Ascent | 2970m/9745ft |
| Maximum Altitude | 849m/2786ft |
| Start/Finish | S/F 1 **Carrick Little car park (///demand.farmer.snuggled).** From Newcastle town centre, follow signs for 'Kilkeel A2'. Head SE out of Newcastle and, after a few miles, pass the Bloody Bridge car park on the left. About 4 miles after Bloody Bridge, TR ('Silent Valley') onto Quarter Road. After 2½ miles on this narrow road, arrive at Carrick Little car park on the right |

The ground underfoot is a mixed bag: some sections use good paths but others are wet and boggy. There are also steep sections where a fall could have serious consequences.

Some start the walk from the Silent Valley Mountain Park but we prefer to start from Carrick Little for two key reasons. Firstly, this enables you to tackle the hardest sections (between Slieve Binnian and Slieve Muck) early on, when you are freshest. Secondly, drinking water is a concern on this long route because there are few watercourses. A start from Carrick Little means that you can replenish your water supply closer to the half-way point: we find that the fast-moving Miners Hole River, near 8, is a good source of water.

Note that confusingly you will climb two different peaks named Slievenaglogh on this route.

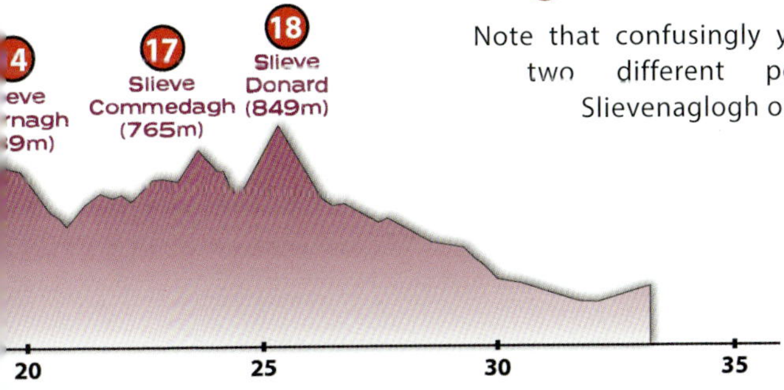

## Water:

Miners Hole River (N of 8)

Slieve Meelmore spring: close to the W side of the MW, SE of 13

Slieve Commedagh spring: close to the S side of the MW, W of 17

*The MW climbing from the Bog of Donard to the summit of Slieve Donard*

## Escape Routes:

Silent Valley Mountain Park (between 5 & 6): the car park and the Head Road are just off the route

Banns Road 8: head S down Banns Road to arrive at a car park beside Moyad Road

Slieve Muck 9: Descend W to Moyad Road

Saddle between Carn and Loughshannagh 12: from the stile head W and then NW to Ott car park on Slievenaman Road

Saddle between 13 and 12: from the stile, descend NW to Happy Valley car park

Hares' Gap 15: descend NW to the Trassey Track and follow it all the way to the Trassey Road

Donard/Commedagh saddle 3: descend NE to Newcastle

Bog of Donard (S of 18): descend E to Bloody Bridge car park

**S/F 1** **See Map 2**. Head N on a track. After 15min, go through a gate and proceed SH on a path running parallel to the MW.

**1** 1.3km: When the path forks, TL and follow a rocky path heading upwards to the NW, parallel to the MW. Where the MW is bisected by another wall, keep SH and continue to follow the MW.

**2** 3.3km: Arrive at a stile, a few hundred metres before the MW terminates at the base of some cliffs. Just afterwards, the path heads to the right, away from the MW, and climbs very steeply towards a cleft in the summit cliffs.

**3** 3.6km: Pass through the cleft and TR to arrive at the summit of **Slieve Binnian (747m)**. Retrace your steps from the summit back to the cleft. Head downhill to the W on a faint path towards the Silent Valley Reservoir. After a few metres, ignore another faint path on the left, which heads (underneath some crags) towards a section of the MW. Instead, continue downhill towards the reservoir. After a minute or so, leave the path and head SW down the grassy slope for a few metres until you pick up another faint path. TL and head towards the base of some boulders to the S. The path passes below some small sections of the MW and afterwards, becomes faint. Clamber down some large boulders: you will now be heading towards Wee Binnian, the rocky peak below to the SW. After a few more minutes, the MW comes into view again and the path brings you towards

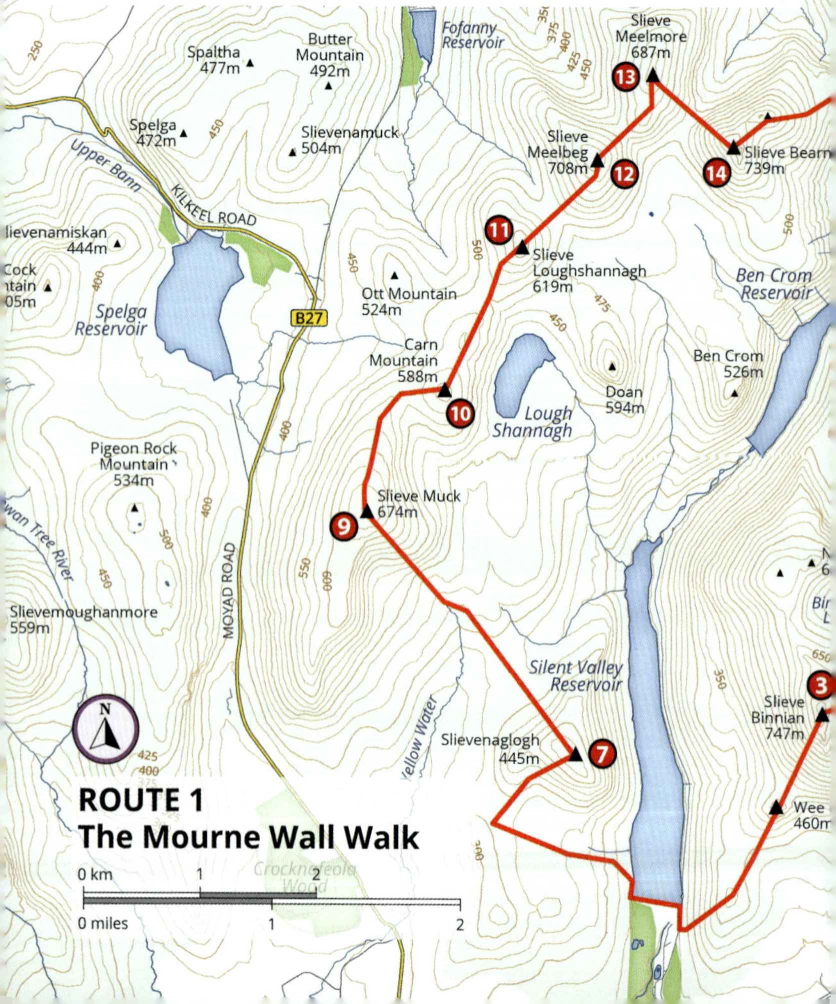


**ROUTE 1**
**The Mourne Wall Walk**

Bryansford
B180
A50
CASTLEWELLAN ROAD
DUNDRUM ROAD
BRYANSFORD ROAD
A2
Shimna River
Tollymore Forest Park
Tipperary Woods
Newcastle
Slievenabrock 437m
Spinkwee River
Glen River
Donard Forest
16
Slievenaglogh 586m
Shan Slieve
17
Slieve Commedagh 765m
Slieve Corragh 641m
Millstone Mountain 460m
18
Slieve Donard 849m
Slieve Beg 596m
Crossone 545m
Cove Mtn 655m
Bloody Bridge River
Bloody Bridge
Slievelamagan 704m
Chimney Rock Mtn 656m
19
Blue Lough
Rocky Mountain 525m
Spences Mountain 517m
Annalong Wood
KILKEEL ROAD
Slieve Binnian East
Annalong River
A2
S/F 1
HEAD ROAD
QUARTER ROAD

it. A few metres from the MW, the path descends steeply over shale, roughly parallel to the wall. Climb over the MW where it re-emerges at a rock slab. Take care here: there are some metal rods, driven into the slab on the other side of the wall, which may help you to scramble down carefully. Now simply follow the wall steeply downhill. At a saddle, cross a stile. Then climb, still alongside the MW.

4 4.8km: When the MW disappears into some rock slabs, climb the last few metres to the summit of **Wee Binnian (460m)**. Head S for a few metres, then SW down through a steep cleft in the rocks. At a small grassy plateau, TR and head N alongside the rocks of the summit, which is just above on the right. Pass through a narrow gap in the rocks and then descend NW for a few metres to pick up a path. TL and follow it, initially SW. The path bends to the left until it heads directly towards the MW again. When you reach the MW, follow it downhill. Cross a saddle and then climb. When the MW bisects another dry-stone wall, pass through a gap in the other wall and continue following the MW, initially W.

5 5.5km: Arrive at the large boulder marking the summit of **Moolieve (332m)**. Continue following the MW, now to the SW. At a stile, cross the MW and continue descending alongside it. At the bottom of the slope, climb another stile: then TR and continue along a path. Shortly afterwards, keep SH at a junction, taking the right fork. After a few minutes, TR and walk along a tarmac lane to the SE tip of the **Silent Valley Reservoir**. TL and walk along the top of the dam at the foot of the reservoir. At the SW corner of the reservoir, TR on a path along the edge of the water. Soon, the path moves away from the reservoir and starts to climb. A few metres afterwards, TR at a junction onto another path and continue climbing. Climb a stile and continue upwards on the path. The path makes a sharp left turn and then climbs to another stile: do not cross it but TR to walk alongside a fence for a few metres until you reach the MW again. Follow the MW upwards: this section can be boggy.

6 8.6km: **See Map 4**. When the MW makes a sharp turn to the right, keep following it. Pass through a gap in another wall and continue steeply uphill alongside the MW. The path here is faint and intermittent and this is a tough climb: at times you will need to clamber over rocks.

7 9.5km: **See Map 2**. Pass a stile and immediately afterwards, when the MW turns sharply left, TL and follow a faint path to the summit cairn of **Slievenaglogh (445m)**. Retrace your steps back to the stile, cross over and follow the MW to the NW. There is a faint path near the wall through the heather. After a level section, descend steeply over rocks. When the route levels again the ground is boggy.

8 10.5km: **See Map 4.** Keep SH across a track known as '**Banns Road**', following the MW. The path becomes rocky and then bends left, away from the MW. After a while, pass through a gap in another dry stone wall. Immediately afterwards, when the path disappears, TR and head to a stile in the MW. TL and climb with the MW on the right. When the MW disappears into rock slabs, skirt around them, well to their left, climbing steeply. You should aim to arrive back at the MW just where the wall re-emerges at the top of the slabs. Then, continue climbing very steeply next to the MW. When the wall disappears for a second time (into some crags), climb up a small steep gully which starts about 30m to the left of the MW. Pick up the MW again and continue climbing.

9 12.5km: From the trig point on the summit of **Slieve Muck (674m)**, head towards two nearby stiles. Climb over the MW on the right-hand stile. Then, TL and follow the MW to the N. **See Map 3**. Just before the MW bends sharply to the right, follow the path to the right, away from the wall, to skirt around a crag. Then continue alongside the MW again, now climbing.

10 14.0km: Arrive at the summit cairn on **Carn Mountain (588m)**. Pass through a gap in another dry-stone wall. Then follow the MW when it bends to the left and heads N. The wall undulates for a while and then climbs quite steeply.

11 15.4km: From the summit of **Slieve Loughshannagh (619m)**, descend to a

saddle and then climb steeply again, still following the MW.

12 16.5km: From the summit of **Slieve Meelbeg (708m)**, descend to another saddle and then climb up the other side. When the MW bisects another dry-stone wall, keep heading uphill (NE).

13 17.5km: Cross a stile at a stone turret built into a corner of the MW. TL to reach the summit cairn of **Slieve Meelmore (687m)**. Cross back over the stile beside the turret and follow the wall SE downhill. Towards the bottom of the slope, the rocks are steep. At a saddle, start climbing, initially alongside the MW. Soon, the path drifts right (up across the slope) and then splits. Take the path furthest to the left (the steepest one) and climb. Now there is a confusing array of different paths: work your way upwards, soon heading back towards the MW again. Arrive back at the MW, just above the point at which it re-emerges at the top of some steep crags. Now climb alongside the MW, working your way up through rocks. Just before the summit, pick up a clear path.

14 18.9km: Arrive at the summit plateau of **Slieve Bearnagh (739m)**. To get to the very top you would need to scramble the last few metres up the rocks on the summit. If you wish to do this then take care. From the summit, follow the MW downhill to the NE. After a few minutes, bear right around some boulders and then follow a path E around the base of the North Tor of Slieve Bearnagh. There are a number of paths here: use the widest one, which is roughly in the middle. The path circles around the North Tor to arrive back at the MW again. Follow the MW steeply downhill. Eventually, the path levels out and skirts to the right of a group of rocks. Afterwards, the path continues to drift away from the MW. When you reach another path, TL and descend steeply on some rock steps.

15 20.0km: Keep SH (NE) past the large cairn at the **Hares' Gap (437m)**. Then climb steeply alongside the MW, to the right of a rocky outcrop.

16 20.9km: **See Map 1**. From the summit cairn on **Slievenaglogh (586m)**, keep following the MW as it undulates along the ridge. Pass over the indistinct summit of **Slieve Corragh (641m)**. Descend briefly and then climb steeply. Cross a stile beside the turret near the summit of Slieve Commedagh: then head NE.

17 23.5km: After a few minutes, arrive at the summit cairn of **Slieve Commedagh (765m)**. Retrace your steps back to the stile: TL and descend SE alongside the MW. Cross a saddle and climb steeply.

18 25.6km: Cross the stile at the summit of **Slieve Donard (849m)**, the highest point in NI. TR and follow the MW downhill (SW), keeping on the E side of it. At the saddle at the **Bog of Donard**, cross a stile and continue S, now with the MW on your left. This section can be boggy.

19 27.9km: **See Map 2**. Where the MW angles to the left, the path bends to the right away from the MW. After a few metres, TL at another path and walk SE. Eventually, arrive at the broad indistinct summit of **Long Seefin (350m)**: this is the last peak of the day although you would hardly notice it was there. Now descend.

20 29.7km: When the MW makes a sharp turn to the right, at a lovely little turret, there are two walls running down to the SW. The most southerly one is the MW but the route is difficult where it heads into trees, so it is easier to follow the more northerly wall. From the turret, clamber down a few large rocks and then follow a path alongside the northerly wall.

21 30.5km: Cross a stile beside an old iron gate. Then TL and walk along a track. After a few minutes, arrive back at the MW which continues to the right. On one side of the wall, there is thick forest and on the other side, there is private land so, unfortunately, this is the last you will see of the MW on this route. Go through a farm gate built into the MW and continue SH on a track. When the track arrives at a road, TR and walk along the road.

S/F 1 33.4: Arrive back at the car park.

# The Seven Sevens

*Views of Slieve Meelbeg*

This iconic challenge walk climbs the seven highest mountains in the Mournes and it owes its existence to a mistake. Only six of those seven summits are more than 700m high: Slieve Meelmore is only 687m. However, earlier versions of OSNI's maps incorrectly showed the height of Meelmore as 704m, leading hikers to believe that there were in fact seven mountains over 700m. And so, the catchy title of the 'Seven Sevens' was born. Although the mapping error has now been corrected, and everyone knows that there are actually only six 'Sevens', the original name persists.

Whilst the MWW has a fixed route, defined as it is by the course of a physical structure, the 7-7s is a more flexible affair. To complete the challenge, you must climb seven mountains: Slieve Donard (849m), Slieve Commedagh (765m), Slieve Binnian (747m), Slieve Bearnagh (739m), Slieve Meelbeg (708m), Slievelamagan (704m) and Slieve Meelmore (687m). As long as you summit each of the seven peaks, the specific routing is up to you. And it is from this flexibility that the challenge derives much of its charm: discussion about the optimal routing is endless and there are many different opinions. For that reason, we describe seven different routes for the 7-7s in this book and there are many other possible itineraries.

Although many will no doubt disagree, in our opinion an anti-clockwise approach is marginally easier than a clockwise one. Hiking anti-clockwise means that you tackle the difficult Ben Crom River section (see below) by descending which is physically easier than climbing up it (which clockwise hikers will have to endure). Furthermore, for the clockwise hiker, Slieve Bearnagh is climbed by the steeper, and more difficult, W approach: anti-clockwise hikers have the advantage of being able to tackle this section by descending.

On the other hand, it is more difficult for anti-clockwise travellers to locate the path on the Ben Crom River section. Furthermore, an anti-clockwise itinerary necessitates a climb of the notoriously rough SW slopes of Slievelamagan: although there is a path indicated on the maps, in practice there is only rough ground of rocks and heather. For this reason, Slievelamagan is perhaps the most maligned mountain in the entire range which is a shame as the views from the summit are sublime. Clockwise hikers will instead descend across this rough ground which is easier.

As the 7-7s has long, exposed sections, it is best saved for a fine day. Mostly you will travel well-trodden paths, often alongside the MW, where navigation in good conditions is straightforward. However, navigation on the ridge between Slievelamagan and the Brandy Pad can be difficult in low visibility or poor weather: there are steep cliffs and a fall could be serious.

The crux of most 7-7s routes is the Ben Crom River section, between 7 & 10, which involves a challenging crossing of the rough, boggy terrain between Ben Crom Reservoir and the foot of Slieve Meelbeg: the ground is consistently wet. These days, a fairly good path runs much of the distance but if you lose it, expect peat hags and a world of pain! As mentioned above, one of the disadvantages of the anti-clockwise routes is that it is harder to find this path from the W: initially, you will need to cross rough ground using navigation skills to locate the path further along. It is easier for clockwise hikers as the path starts right at Ben Crom Reservoir and only disappears as you approach Meelbeg.

The time required to complete the 7-7s depends upon a number of factors: choice of route, fitness, experience, preparation, weather and ground conditions all have a part to play. Many hikers are happy to complete the route in 13hr or more on a long summer day but there are endurance runners who can complete it in well under 4hr. Our advice to first time challengers is not to worry unduly about trying to record the fastest time you are capable of. Simply completing the route in one day is a significant achievement. Enjoy it, get around safely and learn from the experience. If you feel like it, try again in a week or two when you still have good condition: drawing from your previous experience, you will probably record a better time.

# 2 The Seven Sevens: Classic Circuit (anti-clockwise)

This is one of the original and best-known routes for the 7-7s. It is often used for organised races and challenge walks, perhaps because Donard Park in Newcastle, where the route starts and finishes, is well equipped to deal with large numbers of people. However, it is not the easiest of the routes as it is very long. Furthermore, it starts and finishes at sea level so it has more ascent and descent than some of the other routes. Because the route is so often used for challenge hikes and races, we describe it in both directions: Route 2 is the anti-clockwise approach and Route 3 is clockwise. There is much discussion over which of the two is preferable but in our opinion, anti-clockwise is marginally easier (see page 37).

From the summit of Slieve Commedagh, there are two options. We describe below the most popular approach which is to descend to the Brandy Pad (across the rough ground W of the Castles) and then to follow the Brandy Pad W to the Hares' Gap: this requires careful navigation (particularly in low visibility). A safer alternative is simply to continue W from Slieve Commedagh (along the S side of the MW) all the way to the Hares' Gap.

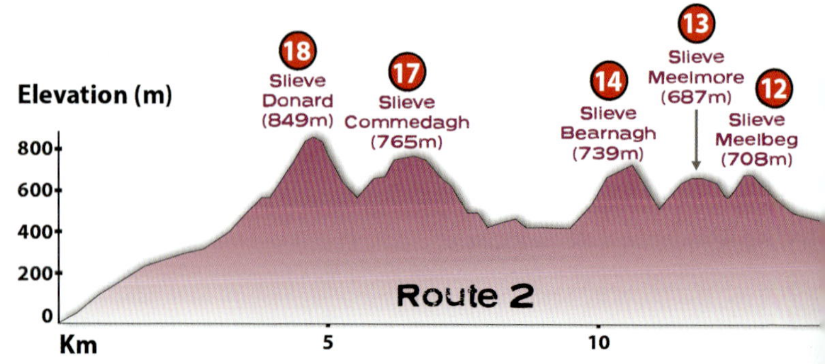

The turret on the summit of Slieve Meelmore

Many claim that this latter approach is slower but we do not think that there is much time difference between the two: although the MW route is probably slightly longer, there is a clear path all the way which allows you to make swift progress.

| | |
|---|---|
| Time (hr) | 4 to 12.5 |
| Distance | 30.6km/19 miles |
| Total Ascent | 2690m/8826ft |
| Maximum Altitude | 849m/2786ft |
| Start/Finish | S/F 2 **Donard car park in Newcastle (///braved.computers.steered).** From Newcastle town centre, follow the signs for 'Donard Forest' or 'Donard Car Park' to arrive at the car park at the S side of the town |

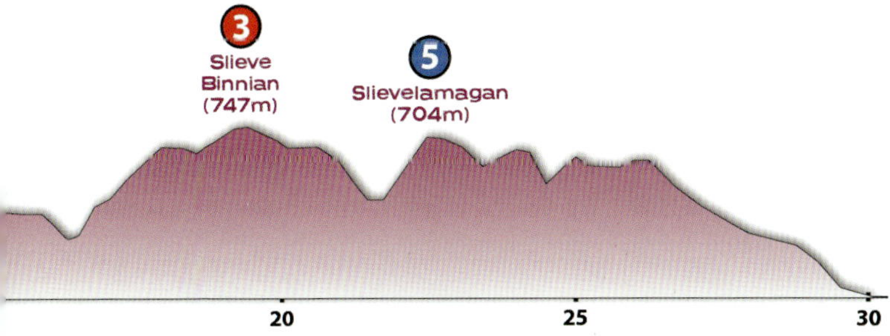

## Water:

Glen River (N of 2)

Slieve Commedagh spring: close to the S side of the MW, a short distance W of 17

Slieve Meelmore spring: close to the W side of the MW, SE of 13

Ben Crom River (between 10 and 8)

## Escape Routes:

Hares' Gap 15: descend NW to the Trassey Track and follow it all the way to the Trassey Road

Saddle between 13 and 12: from the stile, descend NW to Happy Valley car park

Ben Crom Reservoir 7: head S on a tarmac lane all the way to Silent Valley car park

*Heading towards Slieve Bearnagh on the Brandy Pad*

## ROUTE 2
## Seven Sevens: Classic Circuit (anti-clockwise)

ansford
A50
CASTLEWELLAN ROAD
DUNDRUM ROAD
BRYANSFORD ROAD
A2
rest Park
Tipperary Woods
Newcastle
S/F 2
Slievenabrock 437m
Glen River
Donard Forest
Shan Slieve
Slieve Commedagh 765m
17
Millstone Mountain 460m
18
Slieve Donard 849m
Slieve Beg 596m
Crossone 545m
Bloody Bridge River
Bloody Bridge
Chimney Rock Mtn 656m
Rocky Mountain 525m
Spences Mountain 517m
nnalong Wood
Annalong River
KILKEEL ROAD
A2
QUARTER ROAD

S/F 2 **See Map 1**. From the S side of the car park, head W along a tarmac driveway. Almost immediately, go through two gates and continue SW on a gravel track. The track soon bears around to the S and narrows to a gravel path which enters woodland and runs uphill alongside the **Glen River**. After a few minutes, TL and cross **Donard Bridge**. Immediately afterwards, TR and climb a rocky path with the river just on the right. After a few minutes, at a junction, keep SH to climb some steps. Then, continue uphill alongside the river. Ignore other paths branching off to the left.

1 0.9km: TR at a track and cross a large bridge. Immediately afterwards, TL and climb (now with the river on the left). Soon, the path splits but it does not really matter which branch you take as long as you do not stray far from the river. When you arrive at a track, TL and continue to a bridge. Keep heading uphill with the river on the left. Soon afterwards, pass a 19th century ice house on the left.

2 3.3km: The path fords the river and climbs more steeply.

3 3.9km: Arrive at a saddle bisected by the MW (583m): TL and walk uphill (SE) alongside the MW.

18 4.8km: Arrive at the summit of **Slieve Donard (849m)** with its stone turret. This is the highest point in NI. Retrace your steps back to the saddle at 3: then keep SH and climb steeply alongside the MW. From a stone turret, TR and walk NE for a few minutes.

17 6.7km: Arrive at the summit cairn of **Slieve Commedagh (765m)**. Retrace your steps back to the turret: climb over a stile and TR, following the MW NW. Shortly before reaching Slieve Corragh, TL and descend SW down the rough slopes, keeping to the N of a stream. TR onto the **Brandy Pad**. Alternatively, some prefer not to descend directly from Commedagh to the Brandy Pad, and instead continue W alongside the MW all the way to the Hares' Gap.

15 9.6km: From the cairn at the **Hares' Gap (437m)**, follow a path which initially runs SW alongside the MW. The path climbs large stone steps to skirt to the left of some steep cliffs. Shortly after the steps, the path forks: TR to take the rocky path climbing the slope. There are a number of paths which head towards the summit: climb steeply SW, keeping close to the MW. **See Map 3**. Approach the steep cliffs of the **North Tor of Slieve Bearnagh (705m)**. Take a clear path which climbs briefly and then skirts to the left (S) of the North Tor, heading away from the MW. Soon the path heads towards the W. When the path disappears, keep heading W until you arrive close to the MW again: continue to climb alongside it.

14 10.8km: From the rocky outcrops on the summit of **Slieve Bearnagh (739m)**, follow the path around to the W and descend steeply, keeping close to the MW. There are a number of available paths but as long as you keep close to the MW, you should not go wrong. The steep descent is rocky so watch your footing, particularly in the wet. Do not cross over to the N side of the MW where there are steep cliffs. At the bottom of the slope, keep SH across a saddle and climb steeply NW.

13 11.9km: Cross a stile by a turret in a corner of the MW. Immediately afterwards, TL and head briefly S to the summit cairn of **Slieve Meelmore (687m)**. Follow the MW SW downhill. When the MW bisects another dry-stone wall, keep heading downhill to the SW. Descend to a saddle and then climb up the other side.

12 13.0km: From the summit of **Slieve Meelbeg (708m)**, descend SW.

11 13.6km: When you reach a **saddle (511m)**, TL on a path. Shortly afterwards, TL at a fork on a narrow path which contours around the base of Slieve Meelbeg.

10 14.0km: TR and leave the path, descending across rough grass and heather towards the right side of the depression carved out by the **Ben Crom River**. When you reach the river, you should find a path: initially, you can cross to and fro over various little tributaries of the river as there are rough paths on either side. For now, use both sides of the river to your advantage, crossing over when

it is preferable. However, soon the path on the W side of the river becomes better-defined and it makes more sense to use it.

9 15.0km: Cross the river on stones and continue downstream on its E side (on a grassy path).

8 15.8km: At a faint fork where there is a red paint mark on a rock (see image below), bear left (away from the river) on a faint, boggy path. Soon the path bends left around the slopes of Ben Crom and descends steeply.

7 16.6km: **See Map 2**. Climb a stile and cross the walkway over the top of the **Ben Crom Reservoir** dam. Afterwards, TL and climb steeply NE.

6 17.4km: At a **saddle (398m)**, TR (SW) and climb the slopes of Slieve Binnian on a rocky path. It is steep in places and you will need to clamber over a few rocks. Towards the top, the path becomes faint and hard to follow. Head to the right of the large rocky outcrops of the **North Tor (678m)**. Then, follow the path along the crest of the ridge. Approaching the next set of rocky outcrops, the path forks: TR and climb directly towards the outcrops. Head around the left side of the first outcrop. A few minutes later, pass through a gap in a dry-stone wall. Immediately afterwards, TR on a path heading all the way around the right side of another outcrop. Immediately after the outcrop, head back up onto the crest of the ridge: ignore the faint path running SW. Head S along the crest of the ridge.

3 19.7km: Climb through a grassy cleft to arrive at the summit of **Slieve Binnian (747m)**. Retrace your steps back to the saddle at 6.

6 22.1km: At the saddle, continue SH on a path heading NE straight up the slopes of Slievelamagan. Soon the path disappears and unfortunately, there is no easy way up this mountain: you may find sheep tracks here or there but there is no alternative to having to work your way upwards (NE) over the peat and heather, directly towards the summit. In places, this entails clambering over rocks.

5 23.2km: **See Map 1**. From the summit of **Slievelamagan (704m)**, follow a path along the ridge (initially NE). After a few minutes, ignore a path on the right and keep on the wide, rocky path which now descends just to the left of the crest of the ridge. Descend to a **saddle (553m)** and then continue up the slope on the other side. Soon afterwards, TL at an indistinct junction and flank the W slopes of Cove Mountain: there is no need to head all the way to the summit unless you want to. Continue N and descend to another **saddle (507m)**: climb on a wide path on the other side of the saddle. Pass the **Devil's Coachroad**, an aptly named steep gully: watch your footing. The summit of **Slieve Beg (596m)** is a few metres away to the NE. From the summit, head NE on a path which soon descends.

4 25.8km: TR at a large cairn and walk along the **Brandy Pad**. At a fork, TL. Climb to the saddle at 3: cross the stile and retrace your steps to the start.

S/F 2 30.6km: Arrive back at the car park in **Newcastle**.

*The rock at* 8

# 3 The Seven Sevens: Classic Circuit (clockwise)

This itinerary is similar to Route 2 except that it is undertaken in a clockwise direction. It is one of the original and best-known routes for the 7-7s and is often used for organised races and challenge walks: perhaps this is because Donard Park in Newcastle, where the route starts and finishes, is well equipped to deal with large numbers of people. However, it is not the easiest of the routes as it is very long. Furthermore, it starts and finishes at sea level so it has more ascent and descent than some of the other routes.

Take care on the descent from Slieve Commedagh to the Brandy Pad (across the rough ground W of the Castles): this requires careful navigation (particularly in low visibility) to ensure that you do not stray too far E towards the steep cliffs.

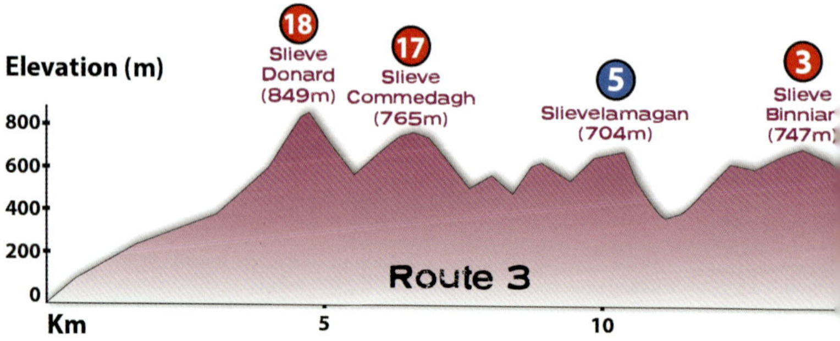

*The incredible views from Slieve Binnian's summit ridge*

| | |
|---|---|
| **Time (hr)** | 4 to 12.5 |
| **Distance** | 30.4km/18.9miles |
| **Total Ascent** | 2690m/0826ft |
| **Maximum Altitude** | 849m/2786ft |
| **Start/Finish** | S/F 2 **Donard car park in Newcastle (///braved.computers.steered)** From Newcastle town centre, follow the signs for 'Donard Forest' or 'Donard Car Park' to arrive at the car park at the S side of the town |

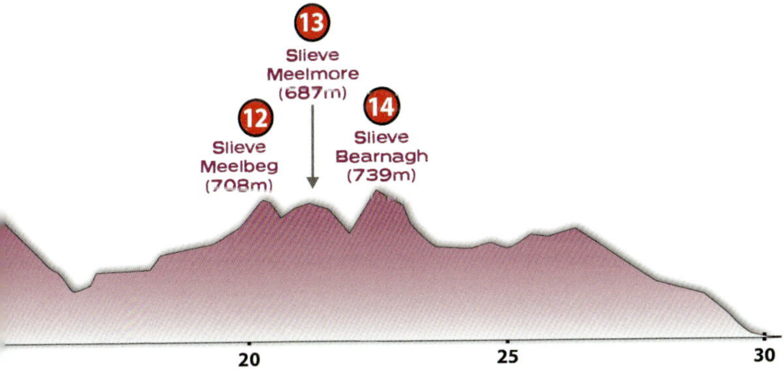

## Water:

Glen River (N of 2)

Ben Crom River (between 10 and 8)

Slieve Meelmore spring: close to the W side of the MW, SE of 13

## Escape Routes:

Ben Crom Reservoir 7: head S on a tarmac lane all the way to Silent Valley car park

Saddle between 13 and 12: from the stile, descend NW to Happy Valley car park

Hares' Gap 15: descend NW to the Trassey Track and follow it all the way to the Trassey Road

*Slieve Commedagh looking divine under a winter sky*

## ROUTE 3
## Seven Sevens: Classic Circuit (clockwise)

nsford
A50
CASTLEWELLAN ROAD
DUNDRUM ROAD
BRYANSFORD ROAD
A2
est Park
Tipperary Woods
Newcastle
S/F 2
Slievenabrock 437m
Glen River
Donard Forest
Shan Slieve
lieve ommedagh 65m
17
18
Millstone Mountain 460m
Slieve Donard 849m
Slieve Beg 596m
Crossone 545m
Mtn 55m
Bloody Bridge River
Bloody Bridge
Chimney Rock Mtn 656m
Rocky Mountain 525m
Spences Mountain 517m
nalong Wood
KILKEEL ROAD
Annalong River
A2
QUARTER ROAD

S/F 2 **See Map 1**. From the S side of the car park, head W along a tarmac driveway. Almost immediately, go through two gates and continue SW on a gravel track. The track soon bears around to the S and narrows to a gravel path which enters woodland and runs uphill alongside the **Glen River**. After a few minutes, TL and cross **Donard Bridge**. Immediately afterwards, TR and climb a rocky path with the river just on the right. After a few minutes, at a junction, keep SH to climb some steps. Then, continue uphill alongside the river. Ignore other paths branching off to the left.

1 0.9km: TR at a track and cross a large bridge. Immediately afterwards, TL and climb (now with the river on the left). Soon, the path splits but it does not really matter which branch you take as long as you do not stray far from the river. When you arrive at a track, TL and continue to a bridge. Keep heading uphill with the river on the left. Soon afterwards, pass a 19th century ice house on the left.

2 3.3km: The path fords the river and climbs more steeply.

3 3.9km: Arrive at a saddle bisected by the MW (583m). TL and walk uphill (SE) alongside the MW.

18 4.8km: Arrive at the summit of **Slieve Donard (849m)** with its stone turret. This is the highest point in NI. Retrace your steps back to the saddle at 3: then keep SH and climb steeply alongside the MW. From a stone turret, TR and walk NE for a few minutes.

17 6.7km: Arrive at the summit cairn of **Slieve Commedagh (765m)**. Retrace your steps back to the turret: climb over a stile and descend SW down the rough slopes, ensuring that you stay W of the steep cliffs of the Castles. Towards the bottom of the slope, aim for a cairn on the **Brandy Pad**.

4 7.6km: From the cairn, head SW up a slope on a rocky path. Keep SH across the summit of **Slieve Beg (596m)**. Shortly afterwards, pass a precipitous gully known as the **Devil's Coachroad**: take care. The path bends right (W) and descends towards a stream bed. Cross the stream bed and climb a steep path to the left of a line of boulders. Eventually, the line of boulders enters a broad rock garden: follow the faint path through the rocks directly up the slope. There is no need to climb all the way to the summit of **Cove Mountain (655m)**: you can skirt around to the right of it if you wish. Soon head SW to a broad saddle, making sure that you avoid the dangerous cliffs to the E. From the saddle, climb S on a rocky path. If you lose the path, keep heading S straight up the slope. Finally, the path bends to the SW.

5 10.2km: At the summit of **Slievelamagan (704m)**, head SW on a faint path which soon disappears. Keep descending steeply SW, working your way in and out of rocks, towards a saddle above Ben Crom Reservoir. There is no easy way down this slope and it is slippery in the wet.

6 11.4km: **See Map 2**. At the saddle, keep SH and climb the slopes of Slieve Binnian on a rocky path. It is steep in places and you will need to clamber over a few rocks. Towards the top, the path becomes faint and hard to follow. Head to the right of the large rocky outcrops of the **North Tor (678m)**. Then, follow the path along the crest of the ridge. Approaching the next set of outcrops, the path forks: TR and climb directly towards the outcrops. Head around the left side of the first outcrop. A few minutes later, pass through a gap in a dry-stone wall. Immediately afterwards, TR on a path heading around the right side of another outcrop. Immediately after the outcrop, head back up onto the crest of the ridge: ignore the faint path running SW. Head S along the crest of the ridge.

3 13.8km: Climb through a grassy cleft to arrive at the summit of **Slieve Binnian (747m)**. Retrace your steps back to the saddle at 6.

6 16.1km: TL at the saddle on a path heading initially NW. After a few minutes, ignore a path on the left. Soon, the main path bends to the SW, descending towards the Ben Crom Reservoir dam: there are a couple of alternative paths but

they seem to interlink. Watch your footing on a few sections of large boulders. Cross the walkway over the top of the **Ben Crom Reservoir** dam.

7 16.9km: At the W side of the dam, cross a stile and TL on a path. Shortly afterwards, TR at a junction and climb on a rocky path. The path eventually levels out and skirts the side of Ben Crom mountain.

8 17.7km: When you reach the **Ben Crom River**, follow it upstream.

9 18.5km: **See Map 3**. Just after a waterfall, cross to the W side of the river and continue upstream on a clear path. After a while, you can cross to and fro over various little tributaries of the river as there are rough paths on either side: use both sides of the river to your advantage, crossing over when it is preferable. As you approach the slopes of Slieve Meelbeg, bear right, climbing away from the river across rough grass and heather: aim towards Slieve Meelbeg.

10 19.5km: Soon TL on a path which contours around the slopes of the mountain.

11 19.8km: Cross a stile at a **saddle (511m)**. Then TR and climb steeply, following the MW.

12 20.4km: From the summit of **Slieve Meelbeg (708m)**, descend to another saddle and then climb up the other side. When the MW bisects another dry-stone wall, keep heading uphill (NE).

13 21.2km: Pass the summit cairn of **Slieve Meelmore (687m)**. Shortly afterwards, TR and cross a stile at a stone turret built into a corner of the MW. Follow the MW SE downhill. Towards the bottom of the slope, the rocks are steep. At a saddle, start climbing, initially alongside the MW. Soon, the path drifts right up across the slope and then splits into a number of paths. Take the path furthest to the left (the steepest one) and climb. Now there is a confusing array of different paths: work your way upwards, soon heading back towards the MW again. Arrive back at the MW, just above the point at which it re-emerges at the top of some steep crags. Now climb alongside the MW, working your way up through rocks. Just before the summit, pick up a clear path.

14 22.6km: From the summit of **Slieve Bearnagh (739m)**, follow the MW downhill to the NE. After a few minutes, bear right around some boulders and then follow a path E around the base of the **North Tor of Slieve Bearnagh**. There are a number of paths here: use the widest one, which is roughly in the middle. The path circles around the North Tor to arrive back at the MW again. Follow the MW steeply downhill. Eventually, the path levels out and skirts to the right of a group of rocks. Afterwards, the path continues to drift away from the MW. When you reach another path, TL and descend steeply on some rock steps.

15 23.7km: **See Map 1**. At the large cairn at the **Hares' Gap (437m)**, TR onto the **Brandy Pad**. Keep SH past the cairn at 4. At a fork, TL. Climb to the saddle at 3: cross the stile and retrace your steps to the start.

S/F 2 30.4km: Arrive back at the car park in **Newcastle**.

# 4 The Seven Sevens: Circuit from Trassey (anti-clockwise)

This route is easier than the Classic Circuits (Routes 2 & 3) because, instead of starting in Newcastle (which is at sea level), it takes advantage of a higher start/finish point and so there is less altitude gain/loss: the car park on Trassey Road is 158m above sea level. We describe an anti-clockwise approach which in our opinion is marginally easier than clockwise (see page 37).

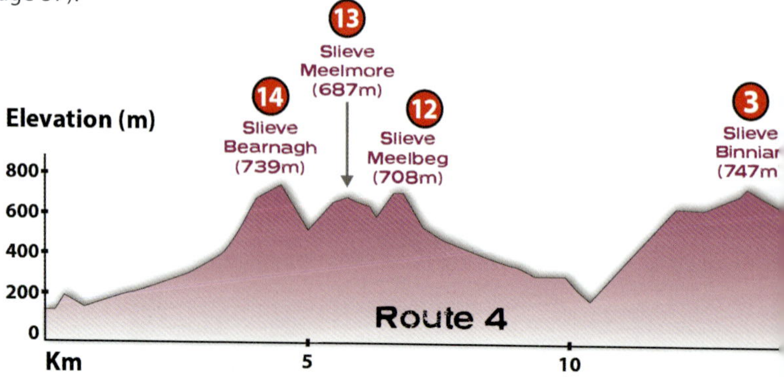

*Slieve Bearnagh viewed from the summit of Slievelamagan*

| Time (hr) | 4 to 12 |
|---|---|
| Distance | 28.9km/18.0miles |
| Total Ascent | 2542m/8340ft |
| Maximum Altitude | 849m/2785ft |
| Start/Finish | S/F 3 **Trassey car park (///aquatic.outhouse.download)** From Newcastle, head NW on Bryansford Road. At Bryansford, TL onto Hilltown Road (B180). After 2.2 miles, TL onto Trassey Road and drive ¾ miles to the car park on the left. If the car park is full, there is additional parking at Meelmore Lodge which is a short distance SW along the Trassey Road: there is a path from Meelmore Lodge which meets the Trassey Track |

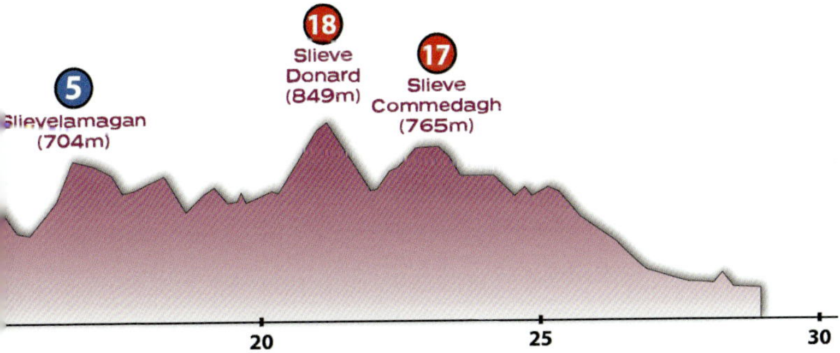

## Water:

Slieve Meelmore spring: close to the W side of the MW, SE of 13

Ben Crom River (between 10 and 8)

Slieve Commedagh spring: close to the S side of the MW, a short distance W of 17

## Escape Routes:

Saddle between 13 and 12: from the stile, descend NW to Happy Valley car park

Ben Crom Reservoir 7: head S on a tarmac lane all the way to Silent Valley car park

Donard/Commedagh saddle 3: descend NE to Newcastle

*Slievelamagan, Cove Mountain & Slieve Beg viewed from Slieve Donard*

**ROUTE 4**
**Seven Sevens: Circuit from Trassey (anti-clockwise)**

nsford
A50
CASTLEWELLAN ROAD
DUNDRUM ROAD
BRYANSFORD ROAD
A2
est Park
Tipperary Woods
Newcastle
Slievenabrock 437m
Glen River
Donard Forest
Shan Slieve
lieve Commedagh 65m
17
Millstone Mountain 460m
18
Slieve Donard 849m
Slieve Beg 596m
Crossone 545m
Mtn 55m
Bloody Bridge River
Bloody Bridge
Chimney Rock Mtn 656m
Rocky Mountain 525m
Spences Mountain 517m
nalong Wood
Annalong River
KILKEEL ROAD
A2
QUARTER ROAD

S/F 3 **See Map 3**. From Trassey car park, TL and head up the road briefly. Just after a house on the left, go through a farm gate onto the broad **Trassey Track**. After 10min, go through another gate. Later, pass through another gate and keep SH on the track.

14 1.9km: Cross a stream and keep SH at a junction (the left fork). Shortly afterwards, TL at another fork. After a few minutes, the sandy track becomes rocky. Keep SH to climb SE up the rocky slope towards a saddle known as the Hares' Gap. The path is intermittent so just work your way upwards SE. Take care on the rocks in the wet.

15 3.3km: Climb a stile over the MW to arrive at the **Hares' Gap (437m)**. At the large cairn, TR and follow a path which initially runs SW alongside the MW. The path climbs large stone steps to skirt to the left of some steep cliffs. Shortly after the steps, the path forks: TR to take the rocky path climbing the slope. There are a number of paths which head towards the summit: climb steeply SW, keeping close to the MW. Approach the steep cliffs of the **North Tor of Slieve Bearnagh (705m)**. Take a clear path which climbs briefly and then skirts to the left (S) of the North Tor, heading away from the MW. Soon the path heads towards the W. When the path disappears, keep heading W until you arrive close to the MW again: continue to climb alongside it.

14 4.5km: From the rocky outcrops on the summit of **Slieve Bearnagh (739m)**, follow the path around to the W and descend steeply, keeping close to the MW. There are a number of available paths but as long as you keep close to the MW, you should not go wrong. The steep descent is rocky so watch your footing, particularly in the wet. Do not cross over to the N side of the MW where there are steep cliffs. At the bottom of the slope, keep SH across a saddle and climb steeply NW.

13 5.6km: Cross a stile by a turret in a corner of the MW. Immediately afterwards, TL and head briefly S to the summit cairn of **Slieve Meelmore (687m)**. Follow the MW SW downhill. When the MW bisects another dry-stone wall, keep heading downhill to the SW. Descend to a saddle and then climb up the other side.

12 6.7km: From the summit of **Slieve Meelbeg (708m)**, descend SW along the MW.

11 7.3km: When you reach a **saddle (511m)**, TL on a path. Shortly afterwards, TL at a fork onto a narrow path which contours around the base of Slieve Meelbeg.

10 7.6km: TR and leave the path, descending across rough grass and heather towards the right side of the depression carved out by the **Ben Crom River**. When you reach the river, you should find a path: initially, you can cross to and fro over various little tributaries of the river as there are rough paths on either side. For now, use both sides of the river to your advantage, crossing over when it is preferable. However, soon the path on the W side of the river becomes better-defined and it makes more sense to use it.

9 8.6km: Cross the river on stones and continue downstream on its E side (on a grassy path).

8 9.4km: At a faint fork where there is a red paint mark on a rock (see page 45), bear left (away from the river) on a faint, boggy path. Soon the path bends left around the slopes of Ben Crom and descends steeply.

7 10.3km: **See Map 2**. Climb a stile and cross the walkway over the top of the **Ben Crom Reservoir** dam. Afterwards, TL and climb steeply NE.

6 11.1km: At a **saddle (398m)**, TR (SW) and climb the slopes of Slieve Binnian on a rocky path. It is steep in places and you will need to clamber over a few rocks. Towards the top, the path becomes faint and hard to follow. Head to the right of the large rocky outcrops of the **North Tor (678m)**. Then, follow the path along the crest of the ridge. Approaching the next set of outcrops, the path forks: TR and climb directly towards the outcrops. Head around the left side of the first outcrop. A few minutes later, pass through a gap in a wall. Immediately

afterwards, TR on a path heading all the way around the right side of another outcrop. Immediately after the outcrop, head back up onto the crest of the ridge: ignore the faint path running SW. Head S along the crest of the ridge.

3 13.4km: Climb through a grassy cleft to arrive at the summit of **Slieve Binnian (747m)**. Retrace your steps back to the saddle at 6.

6 15.8km: At the saddle, continue SH on a path heading NE straight up the slopes of Slievelamagan. Soon the path disappears and unfortunately, there is no easy way up this mountain: you may find sheep tracks here or there but there is no alternative to having to work your way upwards (NE) over the peat and heather directly towards the summit. In places, this entails clambering over rocks.

5 16.9km: **See Map 1**. From the summit of **Slievelamagan (704m)**, follow a path along the ridge (initially NE). After a few minutes, ignore a path on the right and keep on the wide, rocky path which now descends just to the left of the crest of the ridge. Descend to a **saddle (553m)** and then continue up the slope on the other side. Soon afterwards, TL at an indistinct junction and flank the W slopes of Cove Mountain: there is no need to head all the way to the summit unless you want to. Continue N and descend to another **saddle (507m)**: continue on a wide path heading uphill on the other side of the saddle. Pass the **Devil's Coachroad**, an aptly named gully descending steeply through the cliffs to the valley below: watch your footing here. The summit of **Slieve Beg (596m)** is a few metres away to the NE. From the summit, head NE on a path which soon descends.

4 19.5km: TR at a large cairn onto the **Brandy Pad**. At a fork, TL. Climb to the saddle at 3: cross a stile and then TR. Climb steeply uphill (SE) alongside the MW.

18 21.2km: Arrive at the summit of **Slieve Donard (849m)** with its stone turret. This is the highest point in NI. Retrace your steps back to the saddle at 3: then keep SH and climb steeply alongside the MW. From a stone turret, TR and walk NE for a few minutes.

17 23.1km: Arrive at the summit cairn of **Slieve Commedagh (765m)**. Retrace your steps back to the turret: climb over a stile and TR. Head W on a path, following the MW.

15 25.5km: **See Map 3**. Cross a stile over the MW and head NW on a rocky path. This peters out after a few metres and then becomes a faint path which soon runs (NW) just to the right of a shallow grassy gully. Soon the path becomes more clearly defined again. Descend on this path until it passes left into the gully: do not enter the gully but keep SH (NW) on a faint path to the right of it. You will see the Trassey Track far below. It is possible to descend through the gully but this route is more difficult. Soon, the path becomes very muddy in places. Keep heading NW and the path becomes grassy again. Eventually, the grassy path arrives just in front of a small hillock. Ignore the path which leads SH up the hillock: instead, TL and descend to pick up another faint path. Follow the path down to the **Trassey Track**. Then, TR and retrace your steps back to the start.

*The crags on the summit of Slieve Bearnagh*

# 5 The Seven Sevens: Circuit from Carrick Little (anti-clockwise)

Although this route is similar to Route 2, the Classic Circuit (anti-clockwise), it is slightly easier: instead of starting/finishing in Newcastle (which is at sea level), it takes advantage of a higher staging point and so there is less altitude gain/loss. Carrick Little car park is approximately 160m above sea level. We describe an anti-clockwise approach which, in our opinion, is marginally easier than clockwise (see page 37).

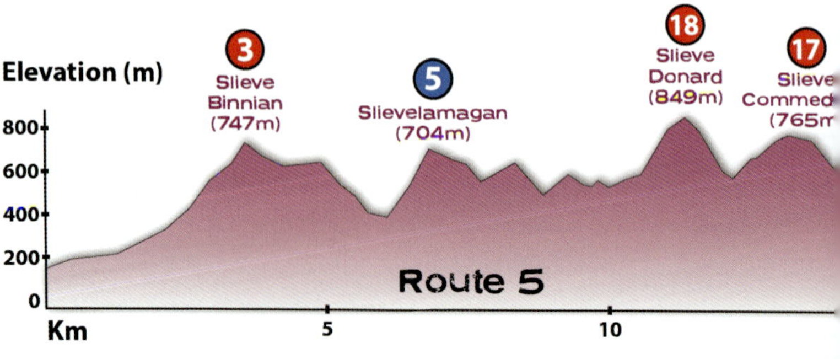

*Slieve Commedagh viewed from the summit of Slieve Corragh*

| | |
|---|---|
| Time (hr) | 4 to 12 |
| Distance | 29.1km/18.1miles |
| Total Ascent | 2540m/8334ft |
| Maximum Altitude | 849m/2786ft |
| Start/Finish | S/F 1 **Carrick Little car park (///demand.farmer.snuggled).** From Newcastle town centre, follow signs for 'Kilkeel A2'. Head SE out of Newcastle and, after a few miles, pass the Bloody Bridge car park on the left. About 4 miles after Bloody Bridge, TR ('Silent Valley') onto Quarter Road. After 2½ miles on this narrow road, arrive at Carrick Little car park on the right |

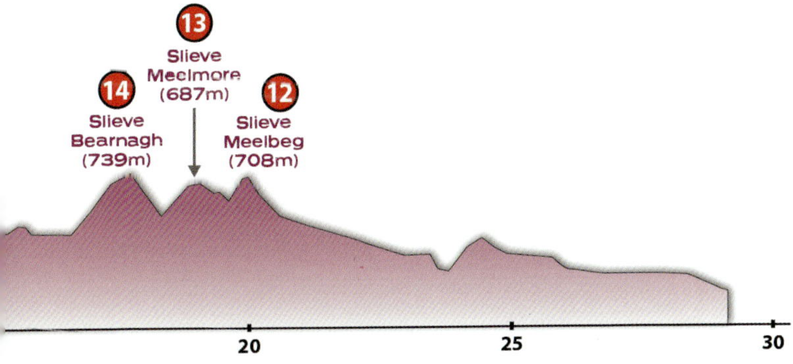

## Water:

Slieve Commedagh spring: close to the S side of the MW, W of 17

Slieve Meelmore spring: close to the W side of the MW, SE of 13

Ben Crom River (between 10 and 8)

Blue Lough (SE of 6)

## Escape Routes:

Donard/Commedagh saddle (3): descend NE to Newcastle

Hares' Gap (15): descend NW to the Trassey Track and follow it all the way to the Trassey Road

Saddle between (13) and (12): from the stile, descend NW to Happy Valley car park

Ben Crom Reservoir (7): head S on a tarmac lane all the way to Silent Valley car park

*The turret near the summit of Slieve Meelmore*

## ROUTE 5
## Seven Sevens: Circuit from Carrick Little (anti-clockwise)

ansford
A50
CASTLEWELLAN ROAD
DUNDRUM ROAD
BRYANSFORD ROAD
A2
rest Park
Tipperary Woods
Newcastle
Slievenabrock 437m
Glen River
Donard Forest
Shan Slieve
Slieve Commedagh 765m
17
Millstone Mountain 460m
18
Slieve Donard 849m
Slieve Beg 596m
Crossone 545m
Bloody Bridge River
Bloody Bridge
Chimney Rock Mtn 656m
Rocky Mountain 525m
Spences Mountain 517m
nnalong Wood
Annalong River
KILKEEL ROAD
A2
QUARTER ROAD
S/F 1

S/F 1 **See Map 2**. Head N on a track. After 15min, go through a gate and proceed SH on a path running parallel to the MW.

1 1.3km: When the path forks, TL and follow a rocky path heading upwards to the NW, parallel to the MW. Where the MW is bisected by another wall, keep SH and continue to follow the MW.

2 3.3km: Arrive at a stile, a few hundred metres before the MW terminates at the base of some cliffs. Just afterwards, the path heads to the right, away from the MW and climbs very steeply towards a cleft in the summit cliffs.

3 3.6km: Pass through the cleft and TR to arrive at the summit of **Slieve Binnian (747m)**. Head N and walk along the crest of the ridge on a path heading towards a series of rocky outcrops. Head around to the left of the first set of outcrops and go through a gap in a dry-stone wall. Keep following the path and eventually, start to climb again. Pass to the left of the last outcrop, the **North Tor (678m)**. Afterwards, the path descends. Shortly before a saddle, take care clambering down a short, but steep, section of rocky steps.

6 5.9km: At the **saddle**, continue SH on a path heading NE straight up the slopes of Slievelamagan. Soon the path disappears and unfortunately, there is no easy way up this mountain: you may find sheep tracks here or there but there is no alternative to having to work your way upwards (NE) over the peat and heather directly towards the summit. In places, this entails clambering over rocks.

5 6.9km: **See Map 1**. From the summit of **Slievelamagan (704m)**, follow a path along the ridge (initially NE). After a few minutes, ignore a path on the right and keep on the wide, rocky path which now descends just to the left of the crest of the ridge. Descend to a **saddle (553m)** and then continue up the slope on the other side. Soon afterwards, TL at an indistinct junction and flank the W slopes of **Cove Mountain**: there is no need to head all the way to the summit unless you want to. Continue N and descend to another **saddle (507m)**: continue on a wide path heading uphill on the other side of the saddle. Pass the **Devil's Coachroad**, a steep gully: watch your footing. The summit of **Slieve Beg (596m)** is a few metres away to the NE. From the summit, head NE on a path which soon descends.

4 9.5km: TR at a large cairn onto the **Brandy Pad**. At a fork, TL. Climb to the saddle at 3: cross a stile and then TR. Climb steeply uphill (SE) alongside the MW.

18 11.2km: Arrive at the summit of **Slieve Donard (849m)** with its stone turret. This is the highest point in NI. Retrace your steps back to the saddle at 3: then keep SH and climb steeply alongside the MW. From a stone turret, TR and walk NE for a few minutes.

17 13.2km: Arrive at the summit cairn of **Slieve Commedagh (765m)**. Retrace your steps back to the turret: climb over a stile and TR. Head W on a path, following the MW NW. Shortly before reaching Slieve Corragh, TL and descend SW down the rough slopes, keeping close to a stream bed. TR onto the **Brandy Pad**. Alternatively, some prefer not to descend directly from Commedagh to the Brandy Pad and instead head W alongside the MW all the way to the Hares' Gap.

15 16.4km: **See Map 3**. From the cairn at the **Hares' Gap (437m)**, follow a path which initially runs SW alongside the MW. The path climbs large stone steps to skirt to the left of some steep cliffs. Shortly after the steps, the path forks: TR to take the rocky path climbing the slope. There are a number of paths which head towards the summit: climb steeply SW, keeping close to the MW. Approach the steep cliffs of the **North Tor of Slieve Bearnagh (705m)**. Take a clear path which climbs briefly and then skirts to the left (S) of the North Tor, heading away from the MW. Soon the path heads towards the W. When the path disappears, keep heading W until you arrive close to the MW again: continue to climb alongside it.

14 17.6km: From the rocky outcrops on the summit of **Slieve Bearnagh (739m)**, follow the path around to the W and descend steeply, keeping close to the MW. There are a number of available paths but as long as you keep close to the MW, you should not go wrong. The steep descent is rocky so watch your footing, particularly in the wet. Do not cross over to the N side of the MW where there are steep cliffs. At the bottom of the slope, keep SH across a saddle and climb steeply NW.

13 18.7km: Cross a stile beside a turret in a corner of the MW. Immediately afterwards, TL and head briefly S to the summit of **Slieve Meelmore (687m)**. Follow the MW SW downhill. When the MW bisects another wall, keep heading downhill to the SW. Descend to a saddle and then climb up the other side.

12 19.8km: From the summit of **Slieve Meelbeg (708m)**, descend SW along the MW.

11 20.4km: When you reach a **saddle (511m)**, TL on a path. Shortly afterwards, TL at a fork onto a narrow path which contours around the base of Slieve Meelbeg.

10 20.7km: TR and leave the path, descending across rough grass and heather towards the right side of the depression carved out by the **Ben Crom River**. When you reach the river, you should find a path: initially, you can cross to and fro over various little tributaries of the river as there are rough paths on either side. For now, use both sides of the river to your advantage, crossing over when it is preferable. However, soon the path on the W side of the river becomes better-defined and it makes more sense to use it.

9 21.8km: Cross the river on stones and continue downstream on its E side (on a grassy path).

8 22.6km: At a faint fork where there is a red paint mark on a rock (see page 45), bear left (away from the river) on a faint, boggy path. Soon the path bends left around the slopes of Ben Crom and descends steeply.

7 23.4km: **See Map 2**. Climb a stile and cross the walkway over the top of the **Ben Crom Reservoir** dam. Afterwards, TL and climb steeply NE.

6 24.3km: Keep SH at the **saddle (398m)** between Slieve Binnian and Slievelamagan, heading SE on a path. Pass **Blue Lough** and continue SE.

1 27.6km: Keep SH on a path. Soon go through the gate passed earlier and head S on a track.

S/F 1 29.1km: Arrive back at the start.

*Heading W off the summit of Slieve Bearnagh*

# 6 The Seven Sevens: Circuit from Ott Car Park (anti-clockwise)

This route is probably the easiest of the 7-7s circuits because it has the highest start/finish point and so there is the least altitude gain/loss: Ott Mountain car park is 379m above sea level. It is also one of the shortest 7-7s routes. We describe it anti-clockwise which in our opinion is marginally easier, however, it could just as easily be hiked clockwise.

There is some rough, boggy ground W of 12, which you must tackle twice: this can be difficult to navigate in low visibility.

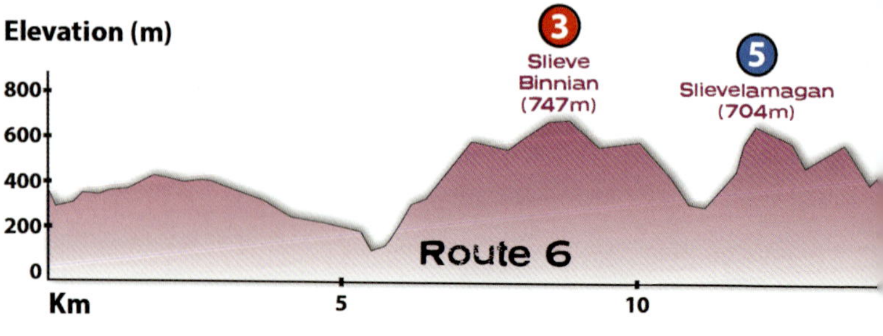

*Ben Crom Reservoir*

| | |
|---|---|
| **Time (hr)** | 3.5 to 12 |
| **Distance** | 28.2km/17.5miles |
| **Total Ascent** | 2321m/7615ft |
| **Maximum Altitude** | 849m/2786ft |
| **Start/Finish** | **S/F 4** **Ott Mountain car park (379m; ///pointed.totally.oxidation)** From Newcastle, head NW on Bryansford Road. At Bryansford, TL onto Hilltown Road (B180). After 3 miles, TL onto Slievenaman Road ('Silent Valley'). After 3½ miles, arrive at the car park on the right |

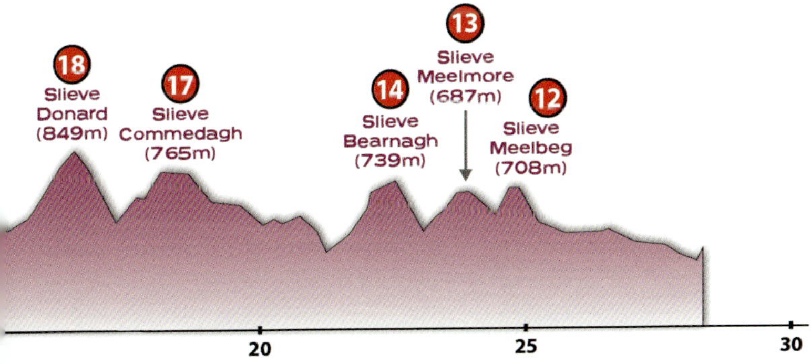

## Water:

Ben Crom River (between 10 and 8)

Slieve Commedagh spring: close to the S side of the MW, W of 17

Slieve Meelmore spring: close to the W side of the MW, SE of 13

## Escape Routes:

Ben Crom Reservoir (7): head S on a tarmac lane all the way to Silent Valley car park

Donard/Commedagh saddle (3): descend NE to Newcastle

Hares' Gap (15): descend NW to the Trassey Track and follow it all the way to the Trassey Road

Saddle between (13) and (12): from the stile, descend NW to Happy Valley car park

*The view S from the Slieve Meelbeg ridge*

## ROUTE 6
## Seven Sevens: Circuit from Ott car park (anti-clockwise)

ansford
A50
CASTLEWELLAN ROAD
DUNDRUM ROAD
BRYANSFORD ROAD
A2
rest Park
Tipperary
Woods
Newcastle
Slievenabrock
437m
Glen River
Donard
Forest
Shan
Slieve
Slieve
Commedagh
765m
17
Millstone
Mountain
460m
18
Slieve Donard
849m
Slieve Beg
596m
Crossone
545m
Mtn
555m
Bloody Bridge River
Bloody
Bridge
Chimney
Rock Mtn
656m
Rocky
Mountain
525m
Spences
Mountain
517m
nnalong
Wood
Annalong River
KILKEEL ROAD
A2
QUARTER ROAD

S/F 4 **See Map 3**. From the car park, walk down the road (NE) for a few metres. Then, cross the road and pick up a stony path heading SE. After a few minutes, TR at a junction of tracks. After 25min, when the rocky path ends, continue SH (E) on a muddy path which is faint in places. Keep roughly E, aiming for the MW.

12 1.8km: Cross a stile over the MW. Then head E on a path. Shortly afterwards, TL at a junction onto a path which contours around the base of Slieve Loughshannagh.

13 2.6km: TR and leave the path, descending ESE across rough ground towards the right side of the depression carved out by the **Ben Crom River**. When you reach the river, you should find a path: initially, you can cross to and fro over various little tributaries of the river as there are rough paths on either side. For now, use both sides of the river to your advantage, crossing over when it is preferable. However, soon the path on the W side of the river becomes better-defined and it makes more sense to use it.

9 3.8km: Cross the river on stones and continue downstream on its E side (on a grassy path).

8 4.6km: At a faint fork where there is a red paint mark on a rock (see page 45), bear left (away from the river) on a faint, boggy path. Soon the path bends left around the slopes of Ben Crom and descends steeply.

7 5.4km: **See Map 2**. Climb a stile and cross the walkway over the top of the **Ben Crom Reservoir** dam. Afterwards, TL and climb steeply NE.

6 6.2km: At a **saddle (398m)**, TR (SW) and climb the slopes of Slieve Binnian on a rocky path. It is steep in places and you will need to clamber over a few rocks. Towards the top, the path becomes faint and hard to follow. Head to the right of the large outcrops of the **North Tor (678m)**. Then, follow the path along the crest of the ridge. Approaching the next set of rocky outcrops, the path forks: TR and climb directly towards the outcrops. Head around the left side of the first outcrop. A few minutes later, pass through a gap in a wall. Immediately afterwards, TR on a path heading all the way around the right side of another outcrop. Immediately after the outcrop, head back up onto the crest of the ridge: ignore the faint path running SW. Head S along the crest of the ridge.

3 8.6km: Climb through a grassy cleft to arrive at the summit of **Slieve Binnian (747m)**. Retrace your steps back to the saddle at 6.

6 11.0km: At the **saddle**, continue SH on a path heading NE straight up the slopes of Slievelamagan. Soon the path disappears and unfortunately, there is no easy way up this mountain: you may find sheep tracks here or there but there is no alternative to having to work your way upwards (NE) over the peat and heather directly towards the summit. In places, this entails clambering over rocks.

5 12.1km: **See Map 1**. From the summit of **Slievelamagan (704m)**, follow a path along the ridge (initially NE). After a few minutes, ignore a path on the right and keep on the wide, rocky path which now descends just to the left of the crest of the ridge. Descend to a **saddle (553m)** and then continue up the slope on the other side. Soon afterwards, TL at an indistinct junction and flank the W slopes of **Cove Mountain**: there is no need to head all the way to the summit unless you want to. Continue N and descend to another **saddle (507m)**: continue on a wide path heading uphill on the other side of the saddle. Pass the **Devil's Coachroad**, a steep gully: watch your footing. The summit of **Slieve Beg (596m)** is a few metres away to the NE. From the summit, head NE on a path which soon descends.

4 14.7km: TR at a large cairn and walk along the **Brandy Pad**. At a fork, TL.

3 15.6km: At a **saddle**, cross a stile and then TR. Climb steeply uphill (SE) alongside the MW.

18 16.5km: Arrive at the summit of **Slieve Donard (849m)** with its stone turret. This is the highest point in NI. Retrace your steps back to the saddle at 3: then keep

SH and climb steeply alongside the MW. From a stone turret, TR and walk NE for a few minutes.

17 18.3km: Arrive at the summit cairn of **Slieve Commedagh (765m)**. Retrace your steps back to the turret: climb over a stile and TR. Head W on a path, following the MW all the way to the Hares' Gap. Alternatively, you can TL shortly before reaching Slieve Corragh and descend SW down the rough slopes, keeping close to a stream: then TR onto the **Brandy Pad** to head to the Hares' Gap.

15 21.3km: **See Map 3**. From the cairn at the **Hares' Gap (437m)**, follow a path which initially runs SW alongside the MW. The path climbs large stone steps to skirt to the left of some steep cliffs. Shortly after the steps, the path forks: TR to take the rocky path climbing the slope. There are a number of paths which head towards the summit: climb steeply SW, keeping close to the MW. Approach the steep cliffs of the **North Tor of Slieve Bearnagh (705m)**. Take a clear path which climbs briefly and then skirts to the left (S) of the North Tor, heading away from the MW. Soon the path heads towards the W. When the path disappears, keep heading W until you arrive close to the MW again: continue to climb alongside it.

14 22.5km: From the rocky outcrops on the summit of **Slieve Bearnagh (739m)**, follow the path around to the W and descend steeply, keeping close to the MW. There are a number of available paths but as long as you keep close to the MW, you should not go wrong. The steep descent is rocky so watch your footing, particularly in the wet. Do not cross over to the N side of the MW where there are steep cliffs. At the bottom of the slope, keep SH across a saddle and climb steeply NW.

13 23.6km: Cross a stile beside a turret in a corner of the MW. Immediately afterwards, TL and head briefly S to the summit cairn of **Slieve Meelmore (687m)**. Follow the MW SW downhill. When the MW bisects another wall, keep heading downhill to the SW. Descend to a saddle and then climb up the other side.

12 24.7km: From the summit of **Slieve Meelbeg (708m)**, descend SW along the MW.

11 25.3km: When you reach a **saddle (511m)**, TL on a path and follow it S around the base of Slieve Loughshannagh.

12 26.6km: Cross the stile passed earlier. Then retrace your steps downhill to the W until you meet the track travelled earlier: follow this downhill to the NW.

S/F 4 28.2km: Arrive back at the start.

*A snowy day on Slieve Donard*

# 7 The Seven Sevens: Linear Route from Carrick Little to Bloody Bridge (clockwise)

This linear route is one of the shortest ways to complete the 7-7s and because you start at Carrick Little car park (160m), you do not have to climb from sea level. Furthermore, the finish at Bloody Bridge means that, unlike most other routes, you do not need to backtrack to descend Slieve Donard. You will also avoid the energy sapping ridge between Slievelamagan and the Brandy Pad. And another advantage is that route-finding along the Ben Crom River section is easier clockwise (see page 37).

There are downsides though: firstly, you will need to climb and descend Slievelamagan by the same route and this means two crossings of the rough and challenging ground SW of the summit. Secondly, although route-finding is easier on the Ben Crom River section, you will have to ascend along it which is physically harder than descending through the tough terrain.

From the Hares' Gap, there are two options. Some prefer to head SE along the Brandy Pad and then TL (before reaching (4)) to climb to the summit of Slieve Commedagh, through the rough terrain to the N. However, the route described here is easier to navigate: simply follow the MW all the way from the Hares' Gap to Slieve Commedagh. Many claim that this latter approach is slower but we do not think that there is a large time difference between the two: the MW route is probably slightly longer but there is a clear path all the way which can be faster than navigating up across rougher ground from the Brandy Pad.

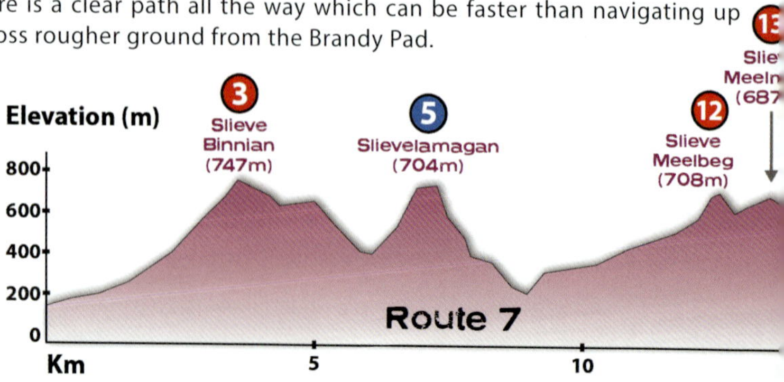

*Doan viewed from the Ben Crom River*

Because the route is linear, you will need to arrange transport of some sort (see 'Accessing start/finish points'). If you are walking in a group, you could leave cars at both ends.

| | |
|---|---|
| **Time (hr)** | 3.5 to 11.5 |
| **Distance** | 25.6km/15.9miles |
| **Total Ascent** | 2340m/7678ft |
| **Maximum Altitude** | 849m/2786ft |
| **Start** | S/F 1 **Carrick Little car park (160m; ///demand.farmer.snuggled)** From Newcastle town centre, follow signs for 'Kilkeel A2'. Head SE out of Newcastle and, after a few miles, pass the Bloody Bridge car park on the left. About 4 miles after Bloody Bridge, TR ('Silent Valley') onto Quarter Road. After 2½ miles on this narrow road, arrive at Carrick Little car park on the right |
| **Finish** | S/F 5 **Bloody Bridge car park (30m; ///sundial.predict.hurricane)** See above |

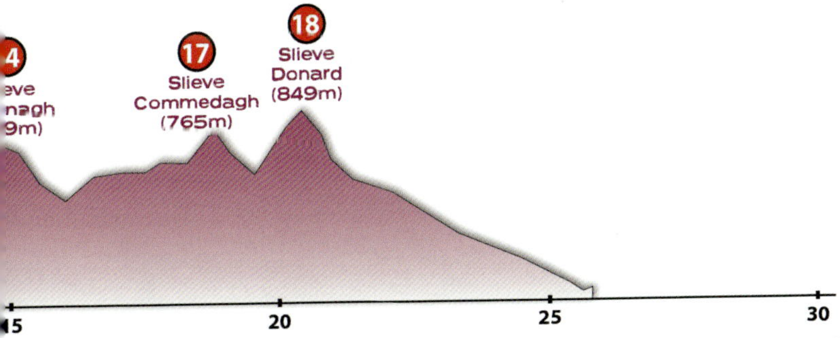

## Water:

Ben Crom River (between 10 and 8)

Slieve Meelmore spring: close to the W side of the MW, SE of 13

Slieve Commedagh spring: close to the S side of the MW, W of 17: you will only pass the spring if you head along the MW between 17 and 15

Bloody Bridge River (E of the Bog of Donard)

## Escape Routes:

Ben Crom Reservoir 7: head S on a tarmac lane all the way to Silent Valley car park

Saddle between 13 and 12: from the stile, descend NW to Happy Valley car park

Hares' Gap 15: descend NW to the Trassey Track and follow it all the way to the Trassey Road

Donard/Commedagh saddle 3: descend NE to Newcastle

*The MW heads across the Hares' Gap and up the slopes of Slieve Bearnagh*

# ROUTE 7
## Seven Sevens: Linear Route from Carrick Little to Bloody Bridge (clockwise)

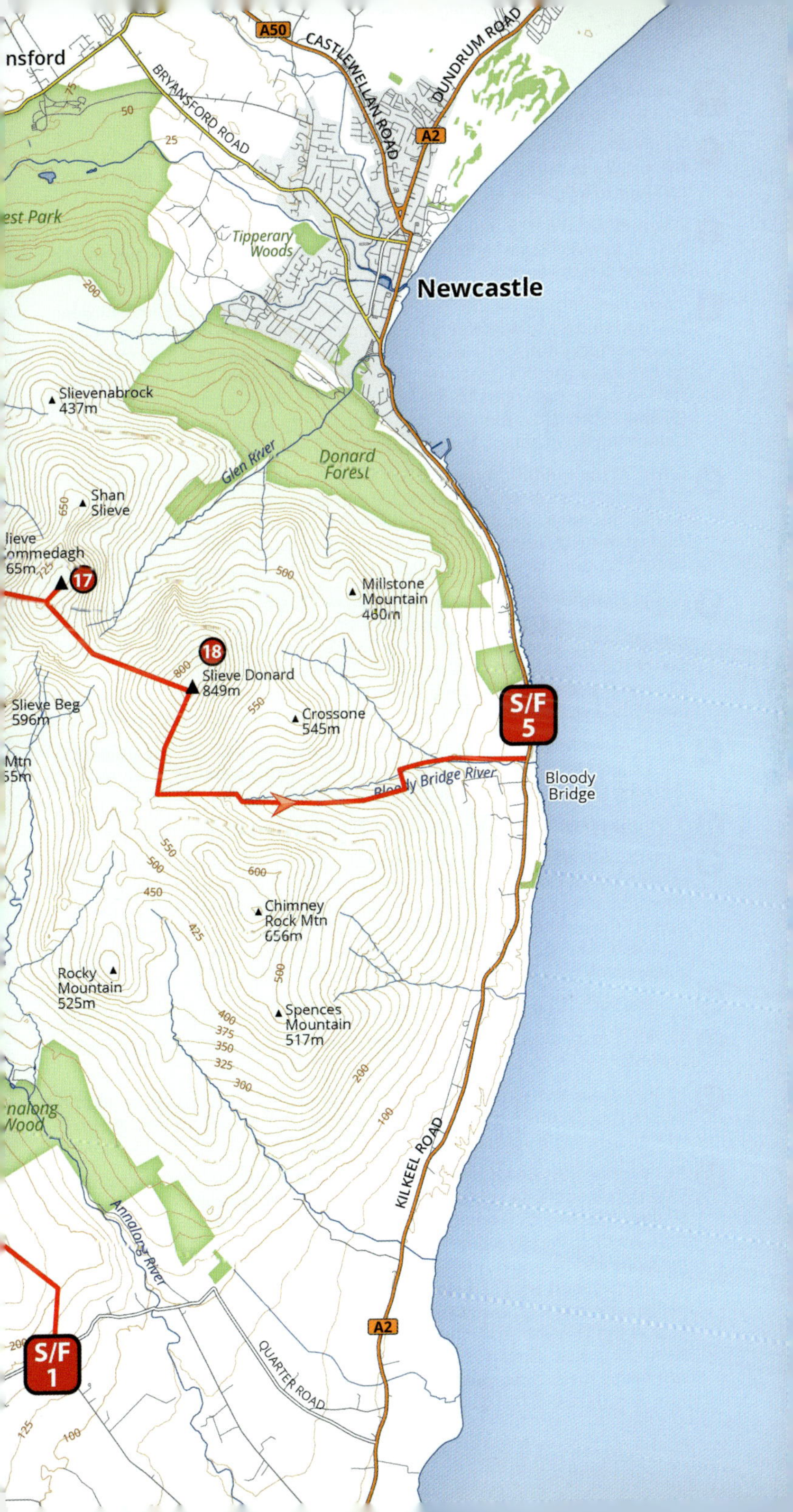
nsford
A50
CASTLEWELLAN ROAD
DUNDRUM ROAD
BRYANSFORD ROAD
A2
est Park
Tipperary Woods
Newcastle
Slievenabrock 437m
Glen River
Donard Forest
Shan Slieve
lieve Commedagh 65m
17
Millstone Mountain 460m
18
Slieve Donard 849m
Slieve Beg 596m
Crossone 545m
S/F 5
Mtn 55m
Bloody Bridge River
Bloody Bridge
Chimney Rock Mtn 656m
Rocky Mountain 525m
Spences Mountain 517m
nalong Wood
Annalong River
KILKEEL ROAD
A2
QUARTER ROAD
S/F 1

S/F 1 **See Map 2**. Head N on a track. After 15min, go through a gate and proceed SH on a path running parallel to the MW.

1 1.3km: When the path forks, TL and follow a rocky path heading upwards to the NW, parallel to the MW. Where the MW is bisected by another wall, keep SH and continue to follow the MW.

2 3.3km: Arrive at a stile, a few hundred metres before the MW terminates at the base of some cliffs. Just afterwards, the path heads to the right, away from the MW, and climbs very steeply towards a cleft in the summit cliffs.

3 3.6km: Pass through the cleft and TR to arrive at the summit of **Slieve Binnian (747m)**. Head N and walk along the crest of the ridge on a path heading towards a series of rocky outcrops. Head around to the left of the first set of outcrops and go through a gap in a dry-stone wall. Keep following the path and eventually, start to climb again. Pass to the left of the last rocky outcrop, the **North Tor (678m)**. Afterwards, the path descends. Shortly before a saddle, take care clambering down a short, but steep, section of rocky steps.

6 5.9km: At the **saddle**, continue SH on a path heading NE straight up the slopes of Slievelamagan. Soon the path disappears and unfortunately, there is no easy way up this mountain: you may find sheep tracks here or there but there is no alternative to having to work your way upwards (NE) over the peat and heather directly towards the summit. In places, this entails clambering over rocks.

5 6.9km: From the summit of **Slievelamagan (704m)**, retrace your steps back to the saddle at 6. At the **saddle**, TR on a path heading initially NW. After a few minutes, ignore a path on the left. Soon, the main path bends to the SW, descending towards the Ben Crom Reservoir dam: there are a couple of alternative paths but they seem to interlink. Watch your footing on sections of large boulders. Cross the walkway over the top of the **Ben Crom Reservoir** dam.

7 8.8km: At the W side of the dam, cross a stile and TL on a path. Shortly afterwards, TR at a junction and climb on a rocky path. The path eventually levels out and skirts the side of Ben Crom mountain.

8 9.7km: **See Map 3**. When you reach the **Ben Crom River**, follow it upstream.

9 10.5km: Just after a waterfall, cross to the W side of the river and continue upstream on a clear path. After a while, you can cross to and fro over various little tributaries of the river as there are rough paths on either side: use both sides of the river to your advantage, crossing over when it is preferable. As you approach the slopes of Slieve Meelbeg, bear right, climbing away from the river across rough grass and heather: aim towards Slieve Meelbeg.

10 11.4km: Soon TL on a path which contours around the slopes of the mountain.

11 11.7km: Cross a stile at a **saddle (511m)**. Then TR and climb steeply, following the MW.

12 12.4km: From the summit of **Slieve Meelbeg (708m)**, descend to another saddle. Then climb up the other side. When the MW bisects another dry-stone wall, keep heading uphill (NE).

13 13.3km: Pass the summit cairn of **Slieve Meelmore (687m)**. Shortly afterwards, TR and cross a stile at a stone turret built into a corner of the MW. Follow the MW SE downhill. Towards the bottom of the slope, the rocks are steep. At a saddle, start climbing, initially alongside the MW. Soon, the path drifts right up across the slope and then splits into a number of paths. Take the path furthest to the left (the steepest one) and climb. Now there is a confusing array of different paths: work your way upwards, soon heading back towards the MW again. Arrive back at the MW, just above the point at which it re-emerges at the top of some steep crags. Now climb alongside the MW, working your way up through rocks. Just before the summit, pick up a clear path.

14 14.5km: From the summit of **Slieve Bearnagh (739m)**, follow the MW downhill to the NE. After a few minutes, bear right around some boulders and then follow a path E around the base of the North Tor of Slieve Bearnagh. There are a number of paths here: use the widest one, which is roughly in the middle. The path circles around the North Tor to arrive back at the MW again. Follow the MW steeply downhill. Eventually, the path levels out and skirts to the right of a group of rocks. Afterwards, the path continues to drift away from the MW. When you reach another path, TL and descend steeply on some rock steps.

15 15.7km: **See Map 1**. Keep SH (NE) past the large cairn at the **Hares' Gap (437m)**: climb steeply alongside the MW, to the right of a rocky outcrop.

16 16.4km: From the summit cairn on **Slievenaglogh (586m)**, keep following the MW as it undulates along the ridge. Pass over the indistinct summit of **Slieve Corragh (641m)**. Descend briefly and then climb steeply. Cross a stile beside the turret near the summit of Slieve Commedagh and walk NE.

17 18.5km: After a few minutes, arrive at the summit cairn of **Slieve Commedagh (765m)**. Retrace your steps back to the stile: TL and descend SE alongside the MW. Cross a saddle and climb steeply.

18 20.3km: TR immediately after the turret on the summit of **Slieve Donard (849m)**, the highest point in NI. Follow the MW downhill (S), keeping on the E side of it. At the saddle at the **Bog of Donard**, TL and head E on a path, keeping close to the base of the valley.

16 22.2km: The path skirts around the left side of an old quarry. After the quarry, continue down to the E on a clear track.

17 24.1km: TL at a junction and pick up a path. Shortly afterwards, cross a stile and descend some stone steps to a track. TL and walk along the track. Ford a river on some large boulders. Immediately afterwards, go SH, briefly uphill: do not descend to the right.

S/F 5 25.6km: Follow the path all the way down to a road. Cross it to arrive at the **Bloody Bridge car park**.

*Looking down the Glen River Valley to Newcastle*

# 8 The Seven Sevens: Linear Route from Ott Car Park to Carrick Little (clockwise)

This is probably the easiest 7-7s route. The distance is the shortest and it has the highest start/finish point so there is less altitude gain/loss than the other routes: Ott car park is 379m above sea level. However, its main selling point is that it avoids the challenging section alongside the Ben Crom River: in fact, it is the only one of our routes that does so. Furthermore, you will climb Slievelamagan by the easier approach from the N, and will therefore have the comparative good fortune of descending (rather than climbing) over the notorious rough ground SW of the summit.

From the Hares' Gap, there are two options. Some prefer to head SE along the Brandy Pad and then TL (before reaching (4)) to climb to the summit of Slieve Commedagh, through the rough terrain to the N. However, the route described here is easier to navigate: simply follow the MW all the way from the Hares' Gap to Slieve Commedagh. Many claim that this latter approach is slower but we do not think that there is a large time difference between the two: the MW route is probably slightly longer but there is a clear path all the way which can be faster than navigating up across rougher ground from the Brandy Pad.

Because the route is linear, you will need to arrange transport of some sort (see 'Accessing start/finish points'). If you are walking in a group, you could leave cars at both ends.

*Slieve Bearnagh and the Hares' Gap*

| | |
|---|---|
| Time (hr) | 3.5 to 10.5 |
| Distance | 23.1km/14.4miles |
| Total Ascent | 2320m/7612ft |
| Maximum Altitude | 849m/2786ft |
| Start | S/F 4 **Ott Mountain car park (379m; ///pointed.totally.oxidation)** From Newcastle, head NW on Bryansford Road. At Bryansford, TL onto Hilltown Road (B180). After 3 miles, TL onto Slievenaman Road ('Silent Valley'). After 3½ miles, arrive at the car park on the right |
| Finish | S/F 1 **Carrick Little car park (160m; ///demand.farmer.snuggled).** From Newcastle town centre, follow signs for 'Kilkeel A2'. Head SE out of Newcastle and, after a few miles, pass the Bloody Bridge car park on the left. About 4 miles after Bloody Bridge, TR ('Silent Valley') onto Quarter Road. After 2½ miles on this narrow road, arrive at Carrick Little car park on the right |

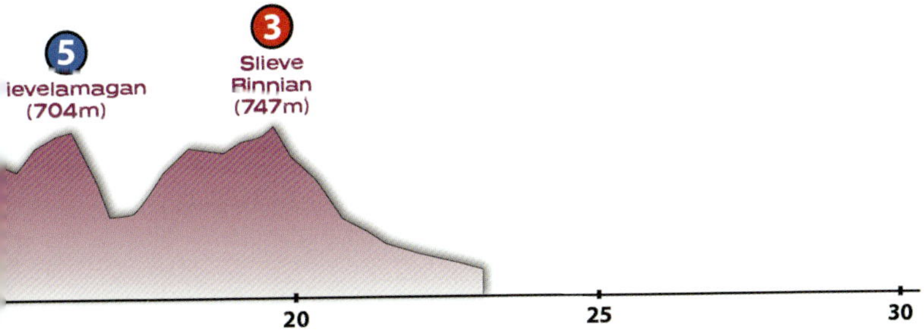

## Water:

Slieve Meelmore spring: close to the W side of the MW, SE of 13

Slieve Commedagh spring: close to the S side of the MW, W of 17. You will only pass the spring if you head along the MW between 17 and 15

## Escape Routes:

Saddle between 13 and 12: from the stile, descend NW to Happy Valley car park

Hares' Gap 15: descend NW to the Trassey Track and follow it all the way to the Trassey Road

Donard/Commedagh saddle 3: descend NE to Newcastle

Saddle at 6: head SE on a path to head directly to Carrick Little car park (without climbing Slieve Binnian)

*The MW heading up to the summit of Slieve Donard*

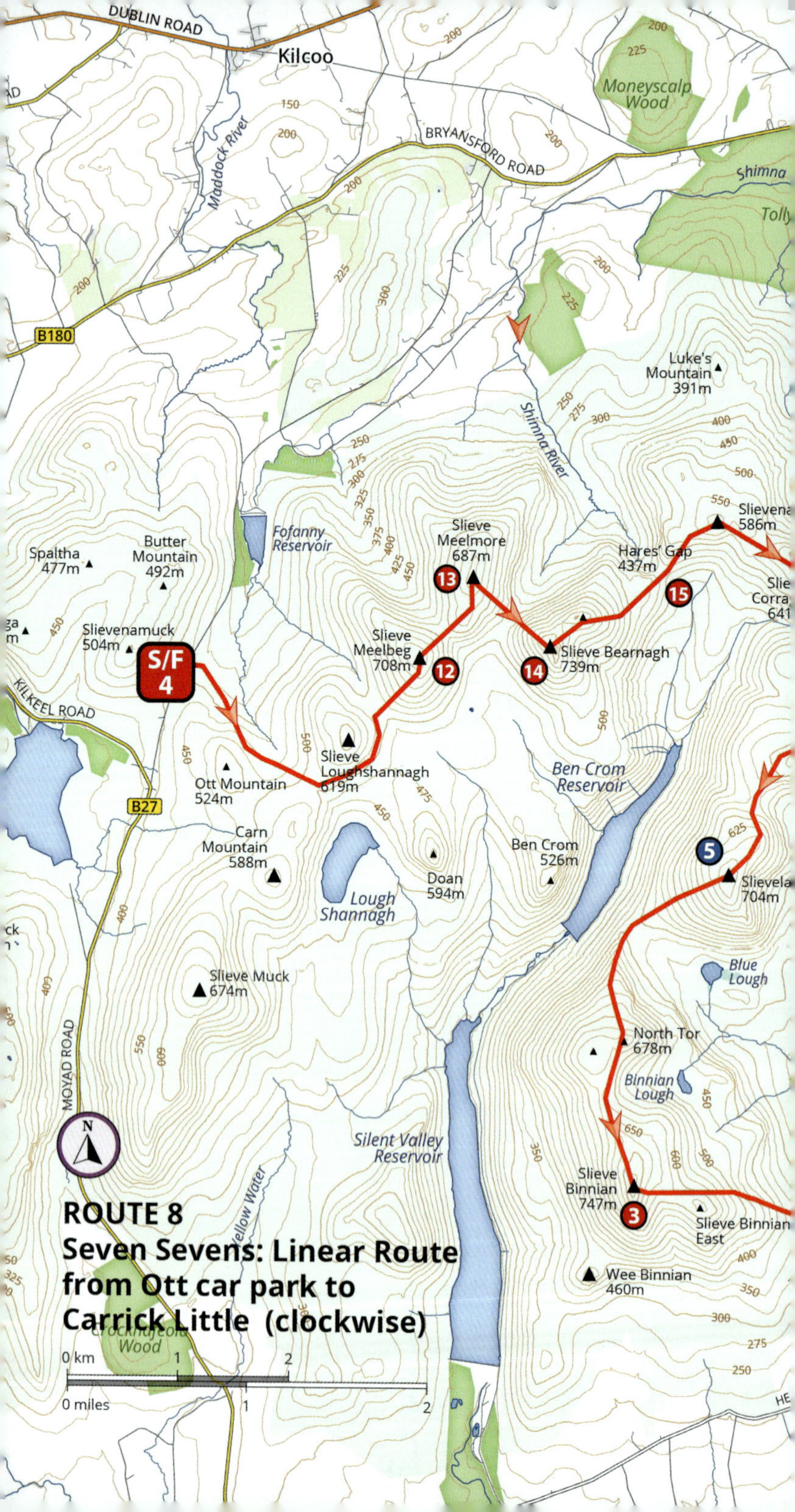


## ROUTE 8
## Seven Sevens: Linear Route from Ott car park to Carrick Little (clockwise)

ansford
A50
CASTLEWELLAN ROAD
DUNDRUM ROAD
BRYANSFORD ROAD
A2
rest Park
Tipperary Woods
Newcastle
Slievenabrock 437m
Glen River
Donard Forest
Shan Slieve
Slieve Commedagh 765m
17
Millstone Mountain 460m
18
Slieve Donard 849m
Slieve Beg 596m
Crossone 545m
e Mtn 655m
Bloody Bridge River
Bloody Bridge
Chimney Rock Mtn 656m
Rocky Mountain 525m
Spences Mountain 517m
nnalong Wood
Annalong River
KILKEEL ROAD
A2
QUARTER ROAD
S/F 1

S/F 4 **See Map 3**. From the car park, walk down the road (NE) for a few metres. Then, cross the road and pick up a stony path heading SE. After a few minutes, TR at a junction of paths. When the rocky path ends, continue SH (E) on a muddy path which is faint in places. Keep roughly E, aiming for the MW.

12 1.8km: Cross a stile over the MW. Then head E on a path. Shortly afterwards, TL at a junction onto a path which contours around the base of Slieve Loughshannagh.

11 2.9km: At a **saddle (511m)**, cross a stile over the MW. Then TR and climb steeply, following the MW.

12 3.6km: From the summit of **Slieve Meelbeg (708m)**, descend to another saddle and then climb up the other side. When the MW bisects another dry-stone wall, keep heading uphill (NE).

13 4.6km: Pass the summit cairn of **Slieve Meelmore (687m)**. Shortly afterwards, TR and cross a stile at a stone turret built into a corner of the MW. Follow the MW SE downhill. Towards the bottom of the slope, the rocks are steep. At a saddle, start climbing, initially alongside the MW. Soon, the path drifts right up across the slope and then splits into a number of paths. Take the path furthest to the left (the steepest one) and climb. Now there is a confusing array of different paths: work your way upwards, soon heading back towards the MW again. Arrive back at the MW, just above the point at which it re-emerges at the top of some steep crags. Now climb alongside the MW, working your way up through rocks. Just before the summit, pick up a clear path.

14 5.8km: From the summit of **Slieve Bearnagh (739m)**, follow the MW downhill to the NE. After a few minutes, bear right around some boulders and then follow a path E around the base of the **North Tor of Slieve Bearnagh**. There are a number of paths here: use the widest one, which is roughly in the middle. The path circles around the North Tor to arrive back at the MW again. Follow the MW steeply downhill. Eventually, the path levels out and skirts to the right of a group of rocks. Afterwards, the path continues to drift away from the MW. When you reach another path, TL and descend steeply on some rock steps.

15 6.9km: Keep SH (NE) past the large cairn at the **Hares' Gap (437m)**. Then climb steeply alongside the MW (to the right of a rocky outcrop).

16 7.7km: **See Map 1**. From the summit cairn on **Slievenaglogh (586m)**, keep following the MW as it undulates along the ridge. Pass over the indistinct summit of **Slieve Corragh (641m)**. Descend briefly and then climb steeply. Cross a stile beside the turret near the summit of Slieve Commedagh and walk NE.

17 9.9km: After a few minutes, arrive at the summit cairn of **Slieve Commedagh (765m)**. Retrace your steps back to the stile: TL and descend SE alongside the MW. Cross the saddle at 3 and climb steeply.

18 11.8km: Arrive at the summit of **Slieve Donard (849m)** with its stone turret. This is the highest point in NI. Retrace your steps back to the saddle at 3: TL and cross a stile. Then follow a path SW. TR onto the **Brandy Pad**.

4 13.5km: TL at a large cairn, heading SW up a slope on a rocky path. Keep SH across the summit of **Slieve Beg (596m)**. Shortly afterwards, pass a precipitous gully known as the **Devil's Coachroad**: take care. The path bends right (W) and descends towards a stream bed. Cross the stream bed and climb a steep path to the left of a line of boulders. Eventually, the line of boulders enters a broad rock garden: follow the faint path through the rocks directly up the slope. There is no need to climb all the way to the summit of **Cove Mountain (655m)**: you can skirt around to the right of it if you wish. Soon head SW to a broad saddle, making sure that you avoid the dangerous cliffs to the E. From the saddle, climb S on a rocky path. If you lose the path, keep heading S straight up the slope. Finally, the path bends to the SW.

5 16.0km: At the summit of **Slievelamagan (704m)**, head SW on a faint path which soon disappears. Keep descending steeply SW, working your way in and

out of rocks, towards a saddle above Ben Crom Reservoir. There is no easy way down this slope and it is slippery in the wet.

6 17.1km: **See Map 2**. At the **saddle**, keep SH and climb the slopes of Slieve Binnian on a rocky path. It is steep in places and you will need to clamber over a few rocks. Towards the top, the path becomes faint and hard to follow. Head to the right of the large rocky outcrops of the **North Tor (678m)**. Then, follow the path along the crest of the ridge. Approaching the next set of outcrops, the path forks: TR and climb directly towards the outcrops. Head around the left side of the first outcrop. A few minutes later, pass through a gap in a dry-stone wall. Immediately afterwards, TR on a path heading all the way around the right side of another rocky outcrop. Immediately after the outcrop, head back up onto the crest of the ridge: ignore the faint path running SW. Head S along the crest of the ridge.

3 19.6km: Climb through a grassy cleft to arrive at the summit of **Slieve Binnian (747m)**. Follow the path S down to a little saddle a few metres away: TL through another cleft in the rocks and then follow a faint path downhill to a dry-stone wall just to the E. TL and follow the wall downhill.

1 21.7km: Keep SH at a junction. Soon go through a gate and then head S on a track.

S/F 1 23.1km: Arrive at the **Carrick Little car park** on **Head Road**.

*A well weathered section of the MW*

## Water:

Glen River (N of ②)

Slieve Commedagh spring: close to the S side of the MW, W of ⑰

Slieve Meelmore spring: close to the W side of the MW, SE of ⑬

Spelga Dam car park (S of ④)

## Escape Routes:

Hares' Gap **15**: descend NW to the Trassey Track and follow it all the way to the Trassey Road

Saddle between **13** and **12**: from the stile, descend NW to Happy Valley car park

Ott Mountain car park **1**

Spelga Dam car park (S of **4**)

*The rocky summit of Hen Mountain*

Drum Lough
DRUMLOUGH ROAD
Upper Bann
HILLTOWN
B8
B25
CROSS ROAD
CASTLEWELLAN ROAD
B180
Hilltown
LEODE ROAD
NEWRY ROAD
Kinnahalla River
Craigdoo
Butter Mountain 492m
Spaltha 479m
4
Spelga 472m
Slievenamuck 504m
Rocky River
S/F 6
Hen Mountain 354m
Slievenamiskan 444m
Upper Bann
KILKEEL ROAD
6
Cock Mountain 505m
Spelga Reservoir
B27
ROSTREVOR ROAD
SANDBANK ROAD
Shankys River
Rocky Mountain 405m
Slieveacarnane
Gruggandoo
Tormanrock 390m
Rowan Tree River
Pigeon Rock Mountain 534m
14
Wee Slievemoughan 428m
MOYAD ROAD
9
Slieve Roe
Slievemoughanmore 559m
Tievedockaragh 473m
12
Eagle Mtn 638m
Shanlieve 626m
Slieve Roosley
Yellow Water River
Aughnaleck River
Crocknafeola Wood
B25
Leckan More
NEWTOWN ROAD
KILBRONEY ROAD
Kilbroney River
Slievemeel 420m
Finlieve 578m
Red Moss River
Rostrevor Forest
Crenville 460m
TULLYFRAME ROAD
SHORE ROAD
Slievemartin 485m
Oak Wood
Slievemeen 472m
Knockchree
Whitewater River
Knockshee 347m
Cassy River
NEWRY ROAD
A2
KILLOWEN ROAD
CORCREAGHAN ROAD

## ROUTES 9 & 10
## Mournes Grand Traverse North & South

0 km 1 2
0 miles 1 2

S/F 2 **See Map 1**. From the S side of the car park, head W along a tarmac driveway. Go through two gates and continue SW on a gravel track. The track soon bears around to the S and narrows to a gravel path, which enters woodland and runs uphill alongside the **Glen River**. After a few minutes, TL and cross **Donard Bridge**. Immediately afterwards, TR and climb a rocky path with the Glen River just on the right. After a few minutes, at a junction, keep SH to climb steps. Then, continue uphill alongside the river. Ignore other paths branching off to the left.

1 0.9km: TR at a track and cross a large bridge. Immediately afterwards, TL and climb on a rocky path, now with the river on the left. Soon, the path splits but it does not really matter which branch you take as long as you do not stray far from the river. When you arrive at a track, TL and continue to a bridge. Here, take a path heading uphill with the river still on the left. Soon afterwards, pass a 19th century ice house on the left: continue climbing on the path, now above the trees.

2 3.3km: The path fords the river and climbs more steeply.

3 3.9km: Arrive at a saddle bisected by the MW (583m): TR and climb steeply alongside the MW until you reach a stone turret at the top of the slope. Then walk NE for a few minutes.

17 4.9km: Arrive at the summit cairn of **Slieve Commedagh (765m)**. Retrace your steps back to the turret: climb over a stile and TR. Proceed along a path to the W, still following the MW.

15 7.6km: **See Map 3**. Descend steeply alongside the MW to the left of a rocky outcrop to arrive at the **Hares' Gap (437m)**. At the large cairn, keep SH and follow a path which initially runs SW alongside the MW. The path climbs large stone steps to skirt to the left of some steep cliffs. Shortly after the steps, the path forks: TR to take the rocky path climbing the slope. There are a number of paths which head towards the summit: climb steeply SW, keeping close to the MW. Approach the steep cliffs of the **North Tor** of **Slieve Bearnagh (705m)**. Take a clear path which climbs briefly and then skirts to the left (S) of the North Tor, heading away from the MW. Soon the path heads towards the W. When the path disappears, keep heading W until you arrive close to the MW again. Continue to climb alongside the MW.

14 8.8km: Arrive at the rocky outcrops on the summit of **Slieve Bearnagh (739m)**. From the summit, follow the path around to the W and descend steeply, keeping close to the MW. There are a number of available paths but as long as you keep close to the MW, you should not go wrong. The steep descent is rocky so watch your footing, particularly in the wet. Do not cross over to the N side of the MW (where there are steep cliffs). At the bottom of the slope, keep SH across a saddle and climb steeply NW.

13 9.9km: Cross a stile beside a turret in a corner of the MW. Immediately afterwards, TL and head briefly S to the summit cairn of **Slieve Meelmore (687m)**. Return to the turret and cross the stile again. Then, TR and follow the wall SW downhill. When the MW bisects another dry-stone wall, keep heading downhill to the SW. Descend to a saddle and then climb up the other side.

12 10.9km: From the summit of **Slieve Meelbeg (708m)**, descend to a saddle and climb the other side. From the summit of **Slieve Loughshannagh (619m)** descend alongside the MW.

12 12.3km: Arrive at another saddle. Cross a stile and head W. Soon, the gradient levels out and then you start climbing the slopes of Ott. From the summit of **Ott Mountain (524m)**, follow a faint path NW along the crest of the wide ridge. When the path disappears, keep heading along the crest (NW and then N) towards a car park which can be seen ahead. Finally, when the ridge descends to a track, TL.

1 14.8km: After a few minutes, cross a road. From the W side of a car park, take a path (initially NW). Soon, cross a stile. Then climb the grassy slope (NW) on a faint path: ignore other paths on the right.

2 15.3km: Just before the top of the slope, TL onto another path and climb the last few metres to the summit of **Slievenamuck (504m)**. From the summit, retrace your steps for a few metres and, when you meet the path of your ascent, keep SH (NE) along a faint grassy path. Ignore paths to the left and right, heading NE until you arrive at a sheep fence. Climb the fence and continue SH on a faint path running NNE alongside, and to the left of, another fence. Ignore waymarks for the Mourne Way heading left.

3 15.8km: Arrive at the indistinct **Butter Mountain (492m)** where there is little to indicate that you are at the summit. Continue N alongside the fence for a few minutes. Descend briefly and then, before a small rise, TL (W) on a faint grassy path which makes its way towards a fence far off to the W. The path soon bends to the NW. If you cannot locate the path then just head NW towards the right side of the fence. Ensure that you do not descend to the N. Just before the fence, TL (SW) onto a faint track and climb briefly. Arrive at a post (with waymarks on it) beside the fence. Climb the fence and proceed W on a faint path. Soon, the path bends to the SW and continues close to the top of the ridge-line. TL at a faint junction of paths: if you cannot locate this junction, simply continue SW, keeping near the top of the ridge.

4 17.5km: From the summit cairn of **Spelga Mountain (472m)**, proceed SE across the grassy slopes, descending towards Spelga Reservoir. Ensure that you do not stray too far to the right (S) where the slope gets much steeper and there are rocky outcrops. When the car park at Spelga Reservoir comes into view, head towards the left (E) side of it. Just before arriving at the main road, ford a stream on some rocks. Be careful as the rocks can be slippery. Immediately afterwards, go through a gate and cross the road. TR and walk W through the car park. At the end of the car park, walk down the road for a few minutes. About 100m after a house on the left, TL along a tarmac lane and arrive at a metal gate: climb the gate and continue towards Spelga Dam. Note that, although this is a popular route, it is not clear whether walkers are actually permitted here. Just in front of the dam, pass through a gate and cross a bridge over the dam run-off canals. Then, proceed on a faint grassy path uphill with the dam towering above you on the left. Soon, rise above the dam: continue SW on the path. After a few minutes, at a rock, the path turns right and heads briefly NW towards a fence. Cross the fence and continue on a path heading initially W up the slope. When the path all but disappears, keep heading straight uphill towards the summit.

5 19.5km: Arrive at the summit of **Slievenamiskan (444m)**. Continue SW on a faint path and descend to a saddle below Cock Mountain. Then, climb SW on a faint path. When the path disappears, continue to work your way broadly SW up the heathery slope towards the summit.

6 20.3: **See Map 6**. Arrive on the N summit of **Cock Mountain (505m)**. From the summit cairn, head W and pick up a faint path. The path soon bends right and descends (NW) on a very steep, heathery slope. It then crosses a saddle and climbs the slopes of Hen Mountain. Next, the path skirts around to the N side of Hen Mountain and climbs to a small saddle between rocky summits: TL and climb SE.

7 21.4: After a few minutes, reach the **S tor of Hen Mountain (354m)**. Return to the saddle and keep SH to climb the **middle tor (361m)**: you will need to scramble up some rocks. Alternatively, TL at the saddle to skirt around the base of the middle tor towards the W tor. From the middle tor, head W to find a path running down to the NW. Near the foot of the slope, TL and walk to the **W tor (337m)**. Pass down through a cleft between the rocks of the W tor and then descend SW on a grassy path. Shortly afterwards, TR onto another path, descending W across the slopes. Go through a gate and walk W on a track.

S/F 6 22.8: Cross the **Sandbank Road** to arrive at a car park.

# 10 The Mournes Grand Traverse (South)

The Mournes Grand Traverse (South) (MGTS) is the sister route of the Mournes Grand Traverse (North) (MGTN; Route 9). You can walk/run the MGTS on its own or combine it with the MGTN, making a mammoth 55km circuit which starts and finishes in Newcastle. For most, the latter option would involve a wild camp somewhere along the way. The MGTS is the harder of the two routes, passing through some of the wildest, least-frequented and most beautiful terrain in the Mournes. It also visits the summit of Doan (which has some of the finest views in the range), scales the challenging peaks of Ben Crom and Slievelamagan, travels part of the famous Brandy Pad and finishes off with an ascent of Slieve Donard, the highest mountain in NI. This is definitely a walk to add to your 'bucket list'.

The terrain is relentless, alternately climbing and descending throughout. The distance and altitude gain/loss are significant. The route has long, exposed sections. There are also long sections without paths, sometimes across wet, boggy ground. Navigation is challenging in places, particularly between Carn and the Ben Crom Reservoir. Also, the ridge between Slievelamagan and the Brandy Pad is a confusing place in low visibility and there are steep cliffs from which a fall would be serious. See the map on pages 98-99.

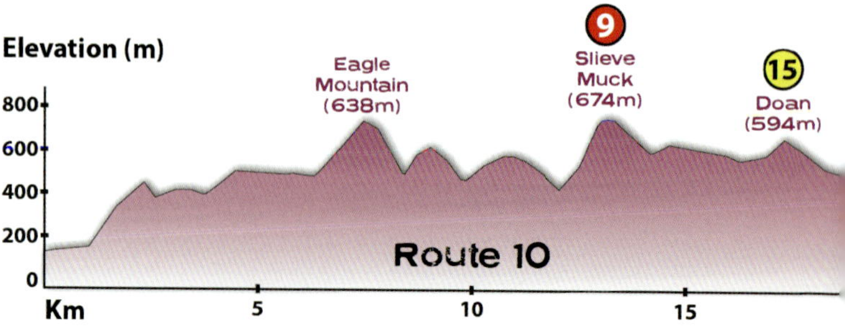

*Slieve Muck viewed from Pigeon Rock Mountain*

| | |
|---|---|
| **Time (hr)** | 4.5 to 14 |
| **Distance** | 32.9km/20.4miles |
| **Total Ascent** | 2449m/8035ft |
| **Maximum Altitude** | 849m/2786ft |
| **Start** | S/F 6 **Sandbank Road car park (///evaded.talents.roadblock)** From Newcastle town centre, follow the signs for 'Bryansford'. At Bryansford, TL and head W on the B180. After 8 miles, TL on Kilkeel Road (B27). After 0.3 miles, TR on Sandbank Road. After 0.7 miles, reach the car park on the right |
| **Finish** | S/F 2 **Donard car park in Newcastle (///braved.computers.steered)** From Newcastle town centre, follow the signs for 'Donard Forest' or 'Donard Car Park' to arrive at the car park at the S side of the town |

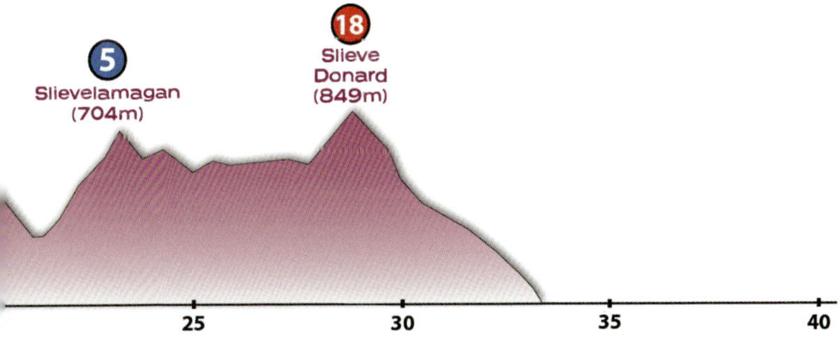

**Water:**

Rocky River (N of 8)

Ben Crom River (between 10 and 8)

Glen River (N of 2)

*Views of the Silent Valley from the summit of Ben Crom*

## Escape Routes:

Saddle S of Rocky Mountain (between 8 & 9): descend W to Leitrim Lodge car park

Pierces Castle 10: follow a track N to Leitrim Lodge car park

Moyad Road (E of 14)

Ben Crom Reservoir 7: head S on a tarmac lane all the way to Silent Valley car park

S/F 6 **See Map 6**. From the car park, cross the road and walk E along a track. After 5-10min, go through a gate and continue S along a track. After 5min, TR at a wooden post, heading SW down a grassy slope directly towards Rocky Mountain: there is no path. At **Rocky River**, walk along the bank to find a safe place to cross: the banks are shallower directly below the summit of Rocky Mountain. Ford the river on boulders which can be slippery. Then, climb straight up grassy slopes towards the summit of Rocky Mountain: again, there is no path and the going is tough.

8 2.4km: At the summit of **Rocky Mountain (405m)**, TL (S) to pick up a grassy path heading down towards a saddle. Head straight across the saddle on a faint path and climb towards some rocky outcrops.

9 3.0km: Pass through the outcrops to arrive at the summit of **Tornamrock (390m)**. Head along the ridge directly towards the pointy peak of Pierces Castle. There is a short section of peat hags to negotiate. Eventually, the path descends to a saddle and continues up the other side. If the path disappears, just keep heading upwards towards the left of the summit outcrops.

10 4.8km: Skirt around the left of the first outcrop and then climb through the rocks to the summit of **Pierces Castle (467m)**. Before the summit, scramble up a steep rock step. Descend SW towards a clear path. Shortly after the route levels off, ignore a track on the left which heads SE. Shortly, TL on a track heading S. After a few minutes, at a crossroad, TL onto a faint path. At another junction, TL and continue S. About 100m before a fence, leave the track (which soon disappears) and proceed SSE towards the fence: try to keep to the firm ground.

11 5.6km: At the fence, TL and walk alongside it. This section is boggy so gaiters are useful. When the fence arrives at a dry-stone wall, climb alongside it. The gradient increases as you climb and the final section is very steep.

12 6.8km: **See Map 5**. Cross the wall to reach the summit cairn of **Shanlieve (626m)**. Then return to the wall and follow it NE: descend to a saddle and then climb up the other side to a stile. **See Map 6**. Now walk briefly SE to the summit cairn of **Eagle Mountain (638m)**. Return to the wall and TR to follow it NW. When the wall bends right, continue to follow it steeply downwards.

13 8.1km: Arrive at a saddle, the **Windy Gap (407m)**, where there are two stiles: cross the left one. Then, TR and climb NE alongside the wall. When the gradient levels, TL (N) and climb to a cairn on top of a rock. From the cairn, head to another large cairn to the NE: this marks the summit of **Slievemoughanmore (559m)**. Head SE and descend to arrive back at the wall again. Then, descend the steep and slippery slope alongside the wall. At a saddle, keep SH and climb NE, still alongside the wall. Follow the wall when it bends to the left.

14 10.5km: Arrive at the summit cairn of **Pigeon Rock Mountain (534m)**. Follow a wall NE downhill. Eventually, cross a stile near a road (B27) and head E towards another stile. Cross the B27 and then climb the stile. Then head uphill (E) alongside a wall.

9 12.6km: After a very steep climb, arrive at the trig point on the summit of **Slieve Muck (674m)**. Just NE of the summit there are two stiles: cross the right-hand one. Then TL and walk alongside the MW, heading N. When the MW bends right, keep following it E.

10 14.0km: **See Map 3**. Climb to the summit of **Carn Mountain (588m)**. Then, keep following the MW as it descends (N). TR at a saddle (510m) and head E on a path. Soon the faint path bears left, contouring around the hillside. Soon, TR on a path, heading SE towards the summit of Doan. Keep SE across a sandy plateau and then climb on a clear path. When the path splits, in front of a false summit (which is just a rocky outcrop), take either path.

15 16.4km: Arrive on the summit of **Doan (594m)** which offers superlative 360° views of the entire Mourne range. Descend from the summit by retracing your steps. TR at the sandy plateau, heading NE.

*The Mourne Wall*

16 17.7km: At the **Ben Crom River**, you should find a path: initially, you can cross to and fro over various little tributaries of the river as there are rough paths on either side. However, soon the path on the W side of the river becomes better-defined and it makes more sense to use it. At 9, cross the river and climb E: you may find a faint path. When the ground levels, bear right and head SE across rough grass and peat hags, keeping to the high ground: it is often boggy. Keep SE and start to climb: you may find a faint path. Arrive on the summit of **Ben Crom (526m)**. Take care as the cliffs to the SE are very steep. Descend by retracing your steps NW. Soon TL and descend S: take care to pass through a gap between crags. At around 350m, you should meet a faint path: TL and follow it SE. After a few minutes, the path bends left to head E

7 20.6km: TR and walk across the top of the dam of **Ben Crom Reservoir**. At the other side of the dam, TL and climb NE on a path.

6 21.7km: At the **saddle (398m)** between Slieve Binnian and Slievelamagan, TL on a path heading NE straight up the slopes of Slievelamagan. Soon the path disappears and unfortunately, there is no easy way up this mountain: you may find sheep tracks here or there but there is no alternative to having to work your way upwards (NE) over the peat and heather directly towards the summit. In places, this entails clambering over rocks.

5 22.5km: **See Map 1**. From the summit of **Slievelamagan (704m)**, follow a path along the ridge (initially NE). After a few minutes, ignore a path on the right and keep on the wide rocky path which now descends just to the left of the crest of the ridge. Descend to a **saddle (553m)** and then continue up the slope on the other side. Soon afterwards, at an indistinct fork, you can go either left or right: the left fork goes directly to the summit of Cove Mountain but the right fork takes you on a thrilling path along the edge of the cliffs to the E of the ridge. The latter is recommended but watch your footing near the cliffs as a fall could have serious consequences. If you take the right fork, eventually the path comes to a dead end: TL and climb directly up the slope (there is no path). From the summit cairn of **Cove Mountain (655m)**, head N to pick up a path. Descend to another saddle: continue on a wide path heading uphill on the other side of it. Pass the Devil's Coachroad, an aptly named gully on the right: watch your footing. The summit of **Slieve Beg (596m)** is a few metres away to the NE. From the summit, head NE on a path which soon descends.

4 25.1km: TR at a large cairn and walk along the **Brandy Pad** which contours around the hillside. At a fork, TR. At the **Bog of Donard**, cross a stile over the MW. Immediately afterwards, TL and walk uphill alongside the MW. The slope gets steeper as you ascend.

18 28.0km: Finally, the slope levels off and you arrive at the summit of **Slieve Donard (849m)**. TL and walk downhill (initially W), still alongside the MW.

3 28.9km: TR at a saddle and descend on a path. At the **Glen River**, continue downhill alongside it. Pass a 19th century ice house. Soon afterwards, TL beside a bridge onto a track. Shortly afterwards, TR and descend on a path: if the path splinters, keep close to the river. TR and cross the next bridge. Immediately afterwards, TL and descend, now to the right of the river. Ignore paths branching off to the right. TL and cross **Donard Bridge**. Immediately afterwards, TR onto a gravel path which later becomes a track.

S/F 2 32.9km: Go through two gates and head E to arrive at the car park in **Newcastle**.

# 11 The Mourne Way

*Spelga Reservoir viewed from the Mourne Way near Slievenamuck*

The Mourne Way is an official waymarked trail between Rostrevor and Newcastle, around the W and N flanks of the Mourne Mountains. It is often overlooked because, with the exception of Spaltha and Slievenamuck, the route does not actually climb over any of the range's summits. However, those who bother to hike it will be treated to views that others miss, particularly on the magnificent section between Leitrim Lodge and the Trassey Track. The route travels the lower ground around the base of the mountains, passing in and out of valleys and over saddles, and therefore provides an entirely different perspective of the Mournes. If you are a well-seasoned Mournes hiker who has not walked this route then you need to rectify that.

The route mainly uses clear paths/tracks which are well marked ('Mourne Way/Ulster Way'). However, between Leitrim Lodge (2) and Rocky Water (3), and between (6) and the summit of Slievenamuck (2), there are sections without paths across rough and/or boggy ground. Some walk or run the entire route in one day but it is lovely to split it into two or more sections, perhaps with a wild camp along the way.

At times, the Mourne Way route marked on the OSNI map does not exactly

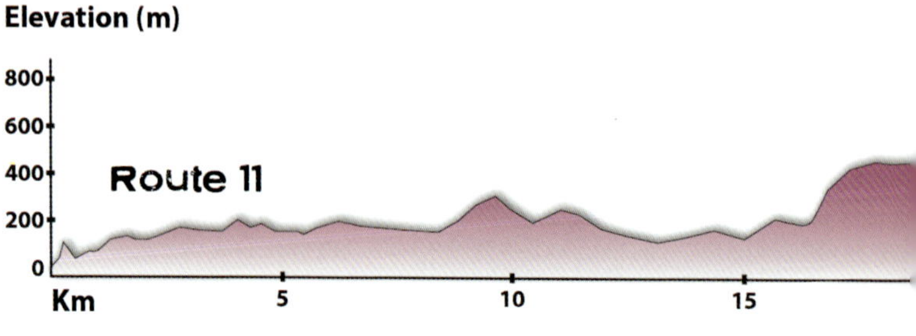

match the actual route on the ground. In Tollymore Forest Park, we have opted for a longer route to that shown on the map so that you get to see more of the park's lovely features and follies.

| | |
|---|---|
| **Time (hr)** | **4 to 12** |
| **Distance** | **40.0km/24.9miles** |
| **Total Ascent** | **1300m/4265ft** |
| **Maximum Altitude** | **504m/1654ft** |
| **Start** | S/F 7 **Kilbroney Park car park (///unveils.flinch.stint)** From Rostrevor, head SE on Shore Road (A2). A few minutes later, TL into Kilbroney Park and follow signs to the main car park |
| **Finish** | S/F 8 **Central Promenade in Newcastle (///padlock.casual.freshest)** |

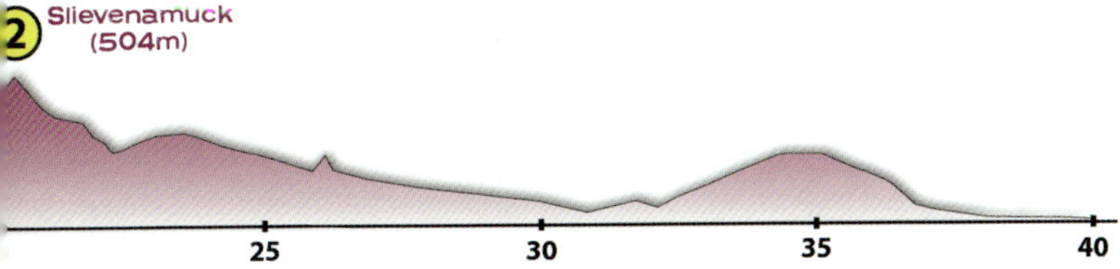

## Water:

- Yellow Water River (1)
- Rocky Water River & Rowan Tree River (3)
- River Bann (between (5) & (6))
- Tollymore Forest Park (between (10) & (11))

## Escape Routes:

Yellow Water River (1)

Leitrim Lodge (2)

Sandbank Road car park: head W on a track from (4)

Spelga Reservoir car park is a short distance SE of the River Bann crossing (between (5) & (6))

Ott Mountain car park (1)

Trassey Track car park (between (9) & (10))

Tollymore Forest Park (between (10) & (11))

*The beautiful farmland along the Mourne Way*

A25
NEWRY ROAD
CASTLEWELLAN ROAD
A25
DUBLIN
HILLTOWN ROAD
Drum Lough
DRUMLOUGH ROAD
Upper Bann
B8
B7
B25
CROSS ROAD
CASTLEWELLAN ROAD
B180
Kinnahalla River
7
Spaltha 479m
Hilltown
LEODE ROAD
NEWRY ROAD
Rocky River
Spelga 472m
B8
Hen Mountain 354m
Slievenamiskan 444m
Upper Bann
KILKEEL ROAD
Cock Mountain 505m
Spelga Reservoir
B27
ROSTREVOR ROAD
SANDBANK ROAD
Shankys River
Rocky Mountain 405m
Slieveacarnane
Gruggandoo
Ballyoully Mountain
2
Tormanrock 390m
Rowan Tree River
Pigeon Rock Mountain 534m
Wee Slievemoughan 428m
MOYAD ROAD
Slieve Roe
Slievemoughanmore 559m
Tievedockaragh 473m
Slieve Roosley
Eagle Mtn 638m
Shanlieve 626m
Yellow Water River
B25
Leckan More
Aughnaleck River
Crocknafeola Wood
KILBRONEY ROAD
Kilbroney River
NEWTOWN ROAD
Slievemeel 420m
Finlieve 578m
Ballymoney Wood
Red Moss River
Rostrevor Forest
Rostrevor
Crenville 460m
S/F 7
TULLYFRAME ROAD
Slievemartin 485m
SHORE ROAD
Oak Wood
Slievemeen 472m
Whitewater River
Knockshee 347m
Cassy River
NEWRY
A2
KILLOWEN ROAD
Carlingford Lough

## ROUTE 11
## The Mourne Way

S/F 7 **See Map 5**. From **Kilbroney Park** car park, follow Mourne Way markers NE though forest.

1 5.2km: Cross a footbridge over the **Yellow Water River**. Immediately afterwards, TL. Shortly afterwards, TR on a track. After crossing a stile, continue NE on a path: look out for an old mass rock on the right.

2 8.8km: **See Map 6**. Ford a stream and then TR at a junction, climbing on a track. Shortly after the track bends right, TL and head E along the N side of a stream bed. Cross a saddle and descend NE on a clear path. When the ground becomes wet and the path becomes faint, aim for a wooden post (with a waymark) down the slope. After the post, a faint grassy path runs to the right of a stream.

3 10.6km: Cross a bridge over **Rocky Water River**. Afterwards, TL on a grassy path which climbs to the Rowan Tree River: TR and follow it upstream. Cross the **Rowan Tree River** at a ford (easy to miss) and pick up a path on the other side. Shortly afterwards, TL on a broad path.

4 13.7km: TR just before a gate heading uphill on a grassy path (parallel to a wall). Follow posts with waymarks clockwise around **Hen Mountain**.

5 15.2km: Ford a stream. Afterwards, TR on a path. Soon start to climb: notice the huge stones beside the path with grooves cut by stonemasons back in the day. TL at a junction (easy to miss) onto a narrow path. After a while, TL and cross a bridge over the **River Bann**. Immediately afterwards, climb on a path. Go through a gate and head diagonally across a road towards a stile. Cross the stile and head N on a path alongside a fence.

6 17.6km: Cross a small stream. Immediately afterwards, TR and climb the steep, grassy slope (no path). There is no waymark indicating this turn: if you reach a larger stream in a deep gully, you have gone too far NE. When you reach the top of the ridge, head NE along it towards a little peak. The ground is boggy: for much of the way there is a faint, grassy path. Reach a small rocky cairn on the summit of **Spaltha (479m)**, where the path forks: take the right branch. Soon, look for a fence to the NE.

7 18.7km: A few hundred metres before the fence, TR on a faint, grassy path (easy to miss) which descends into a shallow valley (filled with peat hags). Keep SH when the path disappears at a particularly boggy section. Afterwards, pick up a faint path which soon runs SW along the top of an old bog road. Just before the path starts its final descent to Spelga Reservoir, TL on a path and climb. When you meet a broad grassy path, TL and climb towards the summit of Slievenamuck.

2 20.9km: Keep SH across the summit of **Slievenamuck (504m)** on a clear path. Shortly afterwards, TR on another path and descend.

1 21.5km: **See Map 3**. Cross a stile and reach **Ott Mountain car park**. TL and walk down the **Slievenaman Road**. Just before a forest, TR, climb a stile and descend on a path. Soon, TL, climb a stile and enter the forest. When the path emerges from the trees again, follow a path N along the E side of **Fofanny Reservoir**. Cross a little bridge and then a stile. Head NE on a grassy path.

8 23.8km: TL at a post and descend on a rocky path. Shortly afterwards, TR at another post. Ford a stream and then cross a stile. Afterwards, follow a dry-stone wall NE.

9 26.1km: TL onto the **Trassey Track**. TR onto the **Trassey Road**. Just afterwards, TR on a track. Soon, TL at a fork. A few minutes later, TR onto a path. After a few more minutes, climb a stone stile and head into **Tollymore Forest Park**.

10 28.6km: **See Map 1**. Turn sharp left at a junction and descend. Cross **Boundary Bridge**. At **Parnell's Bridge**, keep SH following the river.

11 32.0km: TR and cross **Ivy Bridge**. Immediately afterwards, TR on a broad path. Shortly afterwards, turn sharp left at a junction, now climbing. A few minutes later, TR at a junction. Later, TR at a shed. Shortly afterwards, TL at a junction.

12 34.2km: Keep SH at a junction, bearing slightly left (still climbing).

13 35.8km: turn right at a junction, descending gently. 1.3km later, turn sharp right at a junction and continue descending. Climb a gate and keep SH on a lane. Soon keep SH down **Tullybrannigan Road**. TL on **Tipperary Lane**: keep SH when it becomes a path. TL at a road. Just afterwards, TR on a path following a river. TR and cross a footbridge. Shortly afterwards, cross the **Shimna Road** and head E though a park. Soon arrive at **Central Promenade** in **Newcastle**.

*One of the waymarks on the Mourne Way: Cock Mountain is in the background*

# 12 The Mourne 500

All of the previous routes in this book are tough undertakings but the Mourne 500 raises the bar significantly. The aim of the challenge is to summit all of the points in the Mournes which are above 500m and which have more than 10m of prominence above the nearby ground. You are permitted to choose your own route and it will entail a journey of 65-75km with around 4500m of ascent/descent. As with the 7-7s, there is much disagreement over which route is optimal and the route that we have chosen is only one possibility: feel free to tinker with it as you see fit.

Official challengers need to complete the Mourne 500 in less than 20 hours to enter the hall of fame. Furthermore, they must do it unsupported and be completely self-sufficient. Stashing of supplies along the route is forbidden and rightly so: stashed supplies, if abandoned and forgotten, become litter.

However, for mortal hikers who are unconcerned about times, it is a fantastic adventure to hike a Mourne 500 route at a slower pace, purely for enjoyment, wild camping along the way. Or you could break the route down and complete it, section by section, over a series of weeks or months.

The route that we have selected is not the shortest possible one but it has a few advantages. Firstly, it reduces the amount of time spent on country roads after descending Finlieve: many travel directly by road from Sandy Brae to Slieve Binnian. However, in our opinion, it is more pleasant to head more quickly back into the mountains after Finlieve, and overall we do not think that much time is lost by doing so.

Secondly, it allows you to tackle Ben Crom, a tricky little blighter, in the middle of the hike rather than leaving it until close to the end when your stamina reserves are depleted. Thirdly, by heading up the S slopes of Slieve Muck, you avoid having to retrace your steps between Muck's S and N summits.

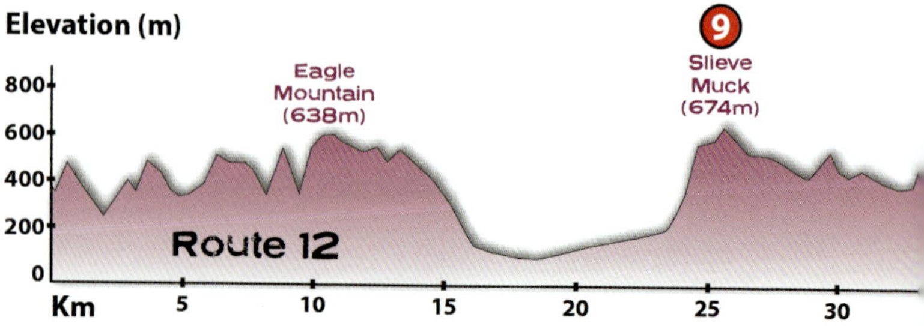

*The summit of Ben Crom*

The terrain is relentless, alternately climbing and descending throughout. The distance and altitude gain/loss are significant. The route has long, exposed sections. There are also long sections without paths, sometimes across wet, boggy ground. The peat hags between Shanlieve and Finlieve are notoriously challenging, particularly after rain. Furthermore, the section between Finlieve and Sandy Brae (across rough ground) is also difficult.

Navigation is sometimes tricky, particularly between Finlieve and Sandy Brae, and between Carn and the Ben Crom Reservoir. Also, the ridge between Slievelamagan and the Brandy Pad is a confusing place in low visibility and there are steep cliffs from which a fall could be serious.

You can find further information on the Mourne 500 at www.mourne500.blogspot.com, including the hall of fame and the rules for undertaking an official challenge.

| | |
|---|---|
| **Time (hr)** | Estimations of time are not useful for such a long route |
| **Distance** | 70.0km/43.5miles |
| **Total Ascent** | 4740m/15552ft |
| **Maximum Altitude** | 849m/2786ft |
| **Start/Finish** | S/F 4 **Ott Mountain car park (379m; ///pointed.totally.oxidation)** From Newcastle, head NW on Bryansford Road. At Bryansford, TL onto Hilltown Road (B180). After 3 miles, TL onto Slievenaman Road ('Silent Valley'). After 3½ miles arrive at the car park on the right |

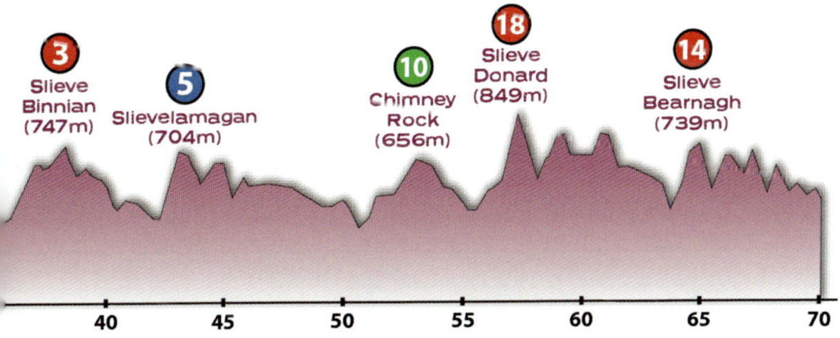

## Water:

Spelga Reservoir car park is a short distance SW of 2

Red Moss/Aughnaleck Rivers (E of 3)

Ben Crom River (between 10 and 8)

Binnian Lough 8

Slieve Commedagh spring: close to the S side of the MW, W of 17

Slieve Meelmore spring: close to the W side of the MW, SE of 13

*The MW crossing both Slieve Meelbeg and Slieve Bearnagh*

## Escape Routes:

Spelga Reservoir car park is a short distance SW of 2

Pigeon Rock Mountain 14: Descend E to Moyad Road

Attical (SE of 4)

Slieve Muck 9: Descend W to Moyad Road

Ben Crom Reservoir 7: head S on a tarmac lane all the way to Silent Valley car park

Saddle at 6: head SE on a path to head directly to Carrick Little car park

Slieve Binnian 3: descend SE to Carrick Little car park

Bog of Donard (S of 18): descend E to Bloody Bridge car park

Donard/Commedagh saddle 3: descend NE to Newcastle

Hares' Gap 15: descend NW to the Trassey Track and follow it all the way to the Trassey Road

Saddle between 13 and 12: from the stile, descend NW to Happy Valley car park

Drum Lough
DRUMLOUGH ROAD
Upper Bann
B8
B25
CROSS ROAD
CASTLEWELLAN ROAD
B180
S/F 4
Kinnahalla River
Hilltown
LEODE ROAD
NEWRY ROAD
Rocky River
Spaltha 479m
Spelga 472m
Slievenamuck 504m
Hen Mountain 354m
Slievenamiskan 444m
Upper Bann
KILKEEL ROAD
Cock Mountain 505m
Spelga Reservoir
B27
ROSTREVOR ROAD
SANDBANK ROAD
Shankys River
Rocky Mountain 405m
Slieveacarnane
Gruggandoo
Ballyoully Mountain
Tormanrock 390m
Pigeon Rock Mountain 534m
Rowan Tree River
Slievemoughanmore 559m
MOYAD ROAD
Slieve Roe
Tievedockaragh 473m
Shanlieve 626m
Eagle Mtn 638m
Slieve Roosley
Yellow Water River
Aughnaleck River
Crocknafeola Wood
Leckan More
KILBRONEY ROAD
Kilbroney River
NEWTOWN ROAD
Slievemeel 420m
Finlieve 578m
Red Moss River
Rostrevor Forest
Crenville 460m
TULLYFRAME ROAD
Slievemartin 485m
SHORE ROAD
Oak Wood
Slievemeen 472m
Knockchree
Whitewater River
Knockshee 347m
Cassy River
A2
KILLOWEN ROAD
NEWRY ROAD
Carlingford Lough
CORCREAGHAN ROAD

ROUTE 12
The Mourne 500

S/F 4 **See Map 6**. From the W side of the car park, take a path initially NW. Cross a stile and climb the grassy slope (NW) on a faint path: ignore other paths on the right.

2 0.6km: Just before the top of the slope, TL onto another path and climb to the summit of **Slievenamuck (504m)**. Descend SW on a clear path towards Spelga Reservoir. At the bottom of the hill, go through a gate and cross a road. TR and walk W through the car park. At the end of the car park, walk down the road for a few minutes. About 100m after a house on the left, TL along a tarmac lane and arrive at a metal gate. Climb the gate and continue towards **Spelga Reservoir Dam**. Note that, although this is a popular route, it is not clear whether walkers are actually permitted here. Just in front of the dam, go through a gate and cross a bridge over the dam run-off canals. Then, head uphill on a faint grassy path beside the dam. Soon, rise above the dam: continue SW on the path. After a few minutes, at a rock, the path turns right and heads briefly NW towards a fence. Cross the fence and continue on a path heading initially W up the slope. When the path all but disappears, keep heading straight uphill towards the summit. At an altitude of about 400m, bear left and work your way W around the S slopes of **Slievenamiskan**: alternatively, you could climb to the summit to bag another peak. From a saddle, climb SW on a faint path. If you lose the path, continue to work your way broadly SW up the heathery slope.

6 3.6km: From the N summit of **Cock Mountain (505m)**, continue SW on a path to descend to a small saddle. Then climb to the **S summit (505m)**. Now head briefly E to descend some rocks. Then, head SE across uneven heathery ground towards the left tip of an old raised bog road which is shaped like an 'L'. Keep to the high ground for as long as you can (the low ground is more boggy). A few hundred metres before the bog road, you should pick up a path which takes you to it. If you cannot locate the path, then simply proceed across the heather to the bog road. TR onto the bog road. After a few minutes, it makes a right-angle turn to the left and continues SE. After a few more minutes, the bog road bends to the right and climbs gently uphill to the S. When the bog road peters out at a grassy plateau, TL and proceed SSE up a grassy slope which gradually increases in gradient. You may find a path from the plateau to the summit of Pigeon Rock but it is patchy. Eventually, when a stile comes into view, make for it.

14 6.1km: Arrive at the cairn on the **N summit of Pigeon Rock Mountain (534m)**. Cross a stile over a wall and TR, following the wall SE. Leave the wall where it makes a 90° turn to the right and head SSE up a slope. After a few minutes, head for a cairn to the S.

1 6.9km: From the **S summit of Pigeon Rock Mountain (534m)**, retrace your steps back to the wall. TL and follow it downhill to the SW. At a saddle, TR and cross a stile over the wall. Then climb steeply SW, still beside the wall. Towards the top of the slope, bear right (leaving the wall) and head NW across open ground.

2 8.7km: From the summit of **Slievemoughanmore (559m)**, head SW towards another cairn on top of a rock. Then head S and return to the wall: follow it SW downhill.

13 9.3km: At the **Windy Gap (407m)**, cross a stile. Then TR and climb steeply SW, now on the S side of the wall. Continue following the wall when it bends sharply to the left. Then, when it bends to the right, keep SH (SE) for a few metres to reach the summit cairn of **Eagle Mountain (638m)**. Return to the wall: TL, following it SW down to a saddle and then up the other side.

12 10.7km: **See Map 5**. When the wall bends right, head S. Shortly, reach the summit cairn on **Shanlieve (626m)**. Head S on a faint path across open ground towards the broad summit of Finlieve. After 10min, the path disappears and you enter possibly the most challenging section of peat hags in the Mournes. If you are undertaking an official Mourne 500 challenge, you will need to pass over the **highest point on the plain (583m)** and so it makes sense to stay near the crest of the ridge to ensure that you do not miss it. However, if you do not care

about ticking off point 583m, it is probably more enjoyable to stay fairly close to the E side of the plain where there are a few trees and the peat hags seem less intimidating. However, take care not to drift too far E as you will lose height.

3 13.2km: **See Map 4**. From the summit of **Finlieve (578m)**, descend E and head across the challenging **Red Bog** to the **Red Moss River**: alternatively, some prefer to head S on one of the old bog roads and then bear left to reach the Red Moss River further E. When you arrive at the river, follow it E: soon there is a faint path. When the path bends right, continue alongside the river. When the river bends left (to head NE), leave it and follow a boundary NE instead.

4 16.1km: Follow a fence which bends left. Then, cross a stream on some boulders. Cross a stile and soon arrive at a lane known as **Sandy Brae**: head S. TL on **Tullyframe Road**. In **Attical**, TL on **Attical Road**.

5 21.1km: Cross **Moyad Road** (B27). Then TR and shortly afterwards, arrive at **Banns Road** car park. Head NE on a wide track bordered by dry-stone walls. Not long after a gate, TL and leave the track, heading NW across rough ground towards a ridge: there are some boggy sections. After crossing the **Yellow Water River**, continue NW, aiming for a steep grassy slope to the right of the crags at the S end of the ridge. Eventually, climb that grassy slope: take great care picking your way through the crags as a fall could be serious. When you reach the top of the ridge, TR and head N along it: take care to avoid the steep cliffs to the E.

6 24.1km: Continue N across the **S summit of Slieve Muck (626m)**.

9 25.3km: From the trig point on the summit of **Slieve Muck (674m)**, head towards two nearby stiles. Climb over the MW on the right-hand stile. Then, follow the MW to the N. Just before the MW bends sharply to the right, follow a path to the right (away from the wall) to skirt around a crag. Then continue alongside the MW again, now climbing.

10 26.7km: **See Map 3**. Arrive at the summit cairn on **Carn Mountain (588m)**. Pass through a gap in another dry-stone wall. Then follow the MW when it bends to the left and heads to the N. Pass over a **rise (557m)**: this is **Carn Mountain (N)** which you must cross for an official challenge.

12 27.6km: At a **saddle (510m)**, TR and head E on a path. Shortly afterwards, TL at a junction on a path which contours around the base of Slieve Loughshannagh. Soon TR onto another path which leads SE up to the summit of Doan.

15 29.2km: From the summit of **Doan (594m)**, retrace your steps NW. From a sandy plateau, TR and head NE. At the **Ben Crom River**, bear right, heading SE. You should find a path: initially, you can cross to and fro over various little tributaries of the river as there are rough paths on either side. For now, you can use both sides of the river to your advantage, crossing over when it is preferable. However, soon the path on the W side of the river becomes better-defined and it makes more sense to use it.

9 31.6km: Cross the river and climb E: you may find a faint path. When the ground levels, bear right and head SE across rough grass and peat hags, keeping to the high ground: it is often boggy. Keep SE and start to climb: you may find a faint path. Arrive on the summit of **Ben Crom (526m)**. Take care as the cliffs to the SE are very steep. Descend by retracing your steps NW. Soon TL and descend S: take care to pass through a gap between crags. At around 350m, you should meet a faint path: TL and follow it SE. After a few minutes, the path bends left to head E.

7 34.3km: TR and walk across the top of the dam of **Ben Crom Reservoir**. At the other side of the dam, TL and climb NE on a path.

6 35.2km: **See Map 2**. At a **saddle (398m)**, TR and climb the slopes of Slieve Binnian on a rocky path. It is steep in places and you will need to clamber over a few rocks. Towards the top, the path becomes hard to follow. Pass just to the W of the large rocky outcrops of the **North Tor (678m)**. Then, follow the path

along the crest of the ridge. Approaching the next set of outcrops, the path forks: TR and climb directly towards the outcrops. Head around the left side of the first outcrop. A few minutes later, pass through a gap in a dry-stone wall. Immediately afterwards, TR on a path heading around the right side of another rocky outcrop. Immediately after the outcrop, head back up onto the crest of the ridge: ignore the faint path running SW. Head S along the crest of the ridge.

3 37.7km: Climb through a grassy cleft to arrive at the summit of **Slieve Binnian (747m)**. Follow the path S down to a little saddle a few metres away: TL through another cleft in the rocks and then follow a faint path downhill to a stile in the MW (just to the E). Cross the stile and head SE towards a small peak.

7 38.4km: From the summit of **Slieve Binnian East** (unnamed on the maps), retrace your steps back to the stile. Cross it and TR following the MW downhill. At an altitude of about 600m, TL and descend N across rough ground.

8 39.7km: From **Binnian Lough**, head N between crags. At the saddle at 6, head NE on a path, straight up the slopes of Slievelamagan. Soon the path disappears and unfortunately, there is no easy way up this mountain: you may find sheep tracks here or there but there is no alternative to having to work your way upwards (NE) over the peat and heather directly towards the summit. In places, this entails clambering over rocks.

5 42.5km: **See Map 1**. From the summit of **Slievelamagan (704m)**, follow a path along the ridge (initially NE). After a few minutes, ignore a path on the right and keep on the wide rocky path which now descends just to the left of the crest of the ridge. Descend to a **saddle (553m)** and then continue up the slope on the other side. Soon afterwards, TL at an indistinct fork. From the summit cairn of **Cove Mountain (655m)**, head N to pick up a path and descend to another saddle: continue on a wide path heading uphill on the other side of the saddle. Pass the **Devil's Coachroad**, a steep gully: watch your footing. The summit of **Slieve Beg (596m)** is a few metres away to the NE. From the summit, head NE on a path which soon descends.

4 45.4km: TR at a cairn onto the **Brandy Pad**. At the **Bog of Donard**, TR and walk along the W side of the MW. This section can be wet and boggy.

19 48.5km: **See Map 2**. Where the MW angles to the left, bear right and head SW up the grassy slopes. Soon, bear left and head S directly towards the summit of Rocky Mountain. From the summit of **Rocky Mountain (525m)**, continue S and descend. After a few minutes, pick up a faint path which descends SE towards a stile over the MW. If you cannot find this path then simply work your way down the slope towards the SE. Make sure that you do not stray too far towards the W as that part of the slope is very steep. Cross the stile and head E on a faint rocky path. After a few minutes, ford **Spences River**. On the other side, there is a choice of paths: ignore the paths running upstream and downstream alongside the river. Instead, head NE and, after a few metres, pick up a faint, grassy path. When the path makes a sudden left turn, climb SE across the slopes.

9 51.1km: From the summit of **Spences Mountain (517m)**, head N across rough ground.

10 52.1km: From the summit of **Chimney Rock Mountain (656m)**, head NW on a path. **See Map 1**. When you reach the **Bog of Donard** again, head NE and contour around the slopes until you reach the summit of **Crossone (545m)**: try not to lose any altitude. Then climb NW up the challenging E slopes of Slieve Donard: aim a little to the N of the summit of Slieve Donard to avoid the steepest slopes. When you are almost at the top, bear left and head SW directly towards the summit.

18 56.4km: From the summit of **Slieve Donard (849m)**, descend NW to the saddle at 3. Then keep SH and climb steeply alongside the MW. From a stone turret, TR and walk NE for a few minutes.

17 58.3km: From the summit cairn of **Slieve Commedagh (765m)**, head N. Shortly afterwards, pass a cairn. Arrive near the edge of some steep cliffs: do not stray too close to the edge. Follow a faint path along the edge of the cliffs until you reach the large cairn on the summit of **Shan Slieve (683m)**. Retrace your steps back to the turret: climb over a stile and TR. Head W on a path beside the MW. You will cross **Slieve Corragh (641m)** and **Slievenaglogh East (573m)**. Continue along the MW. From **Slievenaglogh (586m)**, you will need to climb the MW and head NW to head to Slievenaglogh North.

11 From the summit of **Slievenaglogh North**, retrace your steps. Cross over the MW and TR.

15 62.7km: **See Map 3**. Descend steeply alongside the MW to the left of a rocky outcrop to arrive at the **Hares' Gap (437m)**. Keep SH past the large cairn and follow a path which initially runs SW alongside the MW. The path climbs large stone steps to skirt to the left of some steep cliffs. Shortly after the steps, the path forks. TR to take the rocky path climbing the slope. There are a number of paths which head towards the summit; climb steeply SW. Follow the MW all the way to the point where it meets the **North Tor of Slieve Bearnagh**. Now work your way S around the North Tor. From the W side of the North Tor, head SW alongside the MW again and climb.

14 63.9km: Arrive at a corner of the MW just N of the rocky outcrops on the summit of **Slieve Bearnagh (739m)**. From the summit, follow the path around to the W and descend steeply, keeping close to the MW. There are a number of available paths but as long as you keep close to the MW, you should not go wrong. The steep descent is rocky so watch your footing, particularly in the wet. Do not cross over to the N side of the MW as there are steep cliffs there. At the bottom of the slope, keep SH across a saddle and climb steeply NW.

13 65.1km: Cross a stile beside a turret in a corner of the MW. Immediately afterwards, TL and head briefly S to the summit cairn of **Slieve Meelmore (687m)**. Follow the MW SW downhill. When the MW bisects another wall, keep heading downhill to the SW. Descend to a saddle and then climb up the other side.

12 66.2km: From the summit of **Slieve Meelbeg (708m)**, descend SW along the MW. Cross a **saddle (511m)** and climb.

11 67.1km: From the summit of **Slieve Loughshannagh (619m)**, descend to the saddle at 12. Head W. Soon, the gradient levels out and then you start climbing the slopes of Ott. .

12 68.7km: From the summit of **Ott Mountain (524m)**, follow a faint path NW along the crest of the wide ridge. When the path disappears, keep heading along the crest (NW and then N) towards a car park. Finally, when the ridge descends to a track, TL.

S/F 4 70.0km: Shortly, climb a stile, cross a road and arrive back at the start.

*The summit cairn on Eagle Mountain*

# 13 The Denis Rankin Round (clockwise)

*Slieve Binnian seen from the summit of Doan*

The Denis Rankin Round (DRR) was designed in memory of Denis Rankin, a committed climber and mountain runner who died at the age of 68, while taking part in a mountain race in the Mournes in 2013. It is probably the toughest challenge walk in the Mournes. And it is not simply the terrifying distance (90km), nor the knee destroying altitude gain/loss (approximately 6300m), that makes it so difficult: on the DRR, the terrain itself plays a more significant role than on other challenge walks in the Mournes. As well as summiting all the highest peaks, the challenger must also cross some of the range's lesser-known and least accessible mountains: the terrain around these peaks in the far W of the range is so untamed that few people ever bother trying to climb them. The long grass, deep bogs and impenetrable forest would be tough enough on a normal day-walk but as part of a 90km challenge, they are nothing short of horrific. If that has not put you off then read on!

The aim of the challenge is to summit each of the 39 main summits in the Mournes which are above 400m and which have more than 30m of ascent and descent between them and their neighbours. The summits must be completed (either clockwise or anti-clockwise) in the stipulated order but otherwise, you can choose your own route. Official challengers must complete them within 24hr to become a DRR member and anyone who

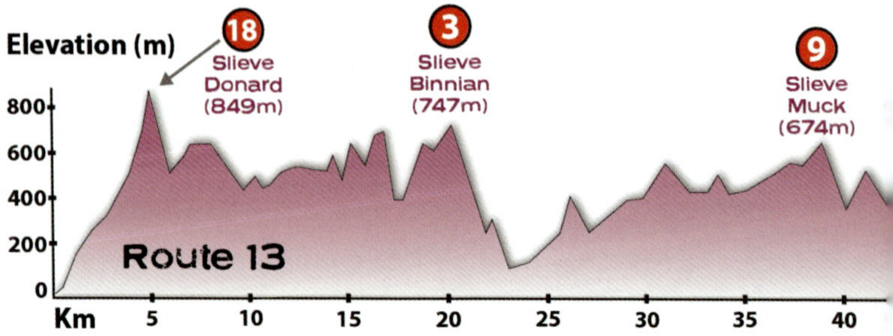

does so is worthy of great respect. The current record holders are Steve Shields (13hr37min) and Aoife Mundow (19hr12min).

Although the completion of the challenge within 24hr might be beyond the abilities of most hikers/runners, there is absolutely no reason why mere mortals, who are unconcerned about times, could not hike the DRR route at a slower pace (just for enjoyment), camping out overnight along the way. It is a wonderful journey and its completion over a number of days would be a fantastic achievement. Or you could break the route down and complete it, section by section, over a series of weeks or months.

The terrain is relentless, alternately climbing and descending throughout. The distance and altitude gain/loss are significant. The route has long, exposed sections. There are also long sections without paths, sometimes across wet, boggy ground. The long section between Shanlieve (12) and Tievedockaragh (9) travels some of the most inhospitable and least-frequented countryside in the Mournes. This is the crux of the DRR even though the mountains there are some of the lowest in the range. Good navigation skills (and a keen sense of humour) are essential. If the ground is wet, it becomes even more difficult. The completion of this part of the DRR is one of the most rewarding achievements in the Mournes.

We describe the route in a clockwise direction although official challengers can also attempt it anti-clockwise. You can find further information on the DRR at www.denisrankinround.com, including the exact waypoints you must pass to successfully complete the challenge, a list of members and the rules for undertaking an official challenge.

| | |
|---|---|
| **Time (hr)** | **Estimations of time are not useful for such a long route** |
| **Distance** | **90.0km/55.9miles** |
| **Total Ascent** | **6300m/20670ft** |
| **Maximum Altitude** | **849m/2786ft** |
| **Start/Finish** | S/F 2 **Donard car park in Newcastle (///braved.computers.steered).** From Newcastle town centre, follow the signs for 'Donard Forest' or 'Donard Car Park' to arrive at the car park at the S side of the town |

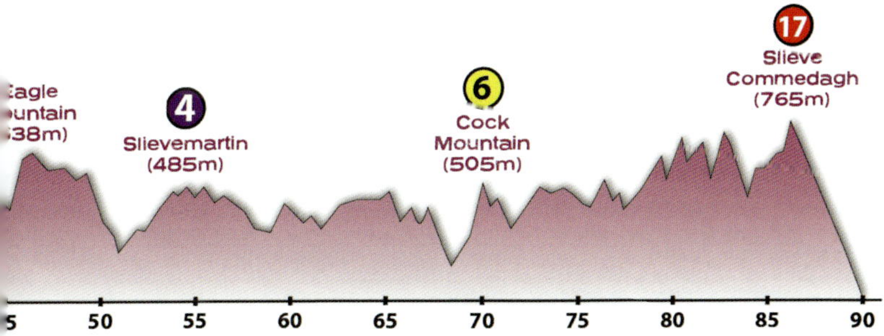

## Water:

Glen River (N of 2)

Miners Hole River (N of 8)

Ben Crom River (between 10 and 8)

Stream at 2

Stream near 7

Rocky River (N of 8)

Spelga Reservoir car park is a short distance SW of 2

Slieve Meelmore spring: close to the W side of the MW, SE of 13

Slieve Commedagh spring: close to the S side of the MW, W of 17

## Escape Routes:

Bog of Donard (S of 18): descend E to Bloody Bridge car park

Silent Valley Mountain Park (between 5 & 6): the car park and the Head Road are just off the route

*The Cooley Mountains viewed from Slievemeen*

Banns Road 8: head S down Banns Road to arrive at a car park beside Moyad Road

Moyad Road (E of 14)

Slievemartin 4 & Slievemeen 3: descend W to Rostrevor

Yellow Water River (between 8 & 9): descend W to Newtown Road

Pierces Castle 10: descend to Leitrim Lodge car park

Rocky River (NE of 8): head NW on a track to Sandbank Road car park

Spelga Reservoir car park is a short distance SW of 2

Ott Mountain car park 1

Saddle between 13 and 12: from the stile, descend NW to Happy Valley car park

Hares' Gap 15: descend NW to the Trassey Track and follow it all the way to the Trassey Road

DRUMLOUGH ROAD
Drum Lough
Upper Bann
B8
B25
CROSS ROAD
CASTLEWELLAN ROAD
B180
Kinnahalla River
Hilltown
LEODE ROAD
NEWRY ROAD
B8
Rocky River
Spaltha 479m
Spelga 472m
Slievenamu 504m
2
Hen Mountain 354m
Slievenamiskan 444m
Upper Bann
KILKEEL ROAD
Cock Mountain 505m
6
Spelga Reservoir
B27
Ott Mour 524m
ROSTREVOR ROAD
SANDBANK ROAD
Shankys River
Slieveacarnane
Gruggandoo
Rocky Mountain 405m
Rowan Tree River
Pigeon Rock Mountain 534m
14
Tormanrock 390m
MOYAD ROAD
Slieve 674m
Slieve Roe
Slievemoughanmore 559m
9
Tievedockaragh 473m
Slieve Roosley
Yellow Water River
Shanlieve 626m
Eagle Mtn 638m
12
B25
Leckan More
KILBRONEY ROAD
NEWTOWN ROAD
Kilbroney River
Aughnaleck River
Crocknafeola Wood
Slievemeel 420m
3
Finlieve 578m
Red Moss River
Rostrevor Forest
Crenville 460m
Attic
TULLYFRAME ROAD
Slievemartin 485m
SHORE ROAD
Oak Wood
3
Slievemeen 472m
Knockchree
Whitewater River
Knockshee 347m
Cassy River
A2
KILLOWEN ROAD
NEWRY ROAD
CORCREAGHAN ROAD

# ROUTE 13
## The Denis Rankin Round

## Stage 1

S/F 2 **See Map 1**. Start at the main entrance to the car park. Head W along a tarmac driveway. Almost immediately, go through two gates and continue SW on a gravel track. The track soon bears around to the S and narrows to a gravel path which enters woodland and runs uphill alongside the **Glen River**. After a few minutes, TL and cross **Donard Bridge**. Immediately afterwards, TR and climb a rocky path with the river just on the right. After a few minutes, at a junction, keep SH to climb some steps. Then, continue uphill alongside the river. Ignore other paths branching off to the left.

1 0.9km: TR at a track and cross a large bridge. Immediately afterwards, TL and climb (now with the river on the left). Soon, the path splits but it does not really matter which branch you take as long as you do not stray far from the river. When you arrive at a track, TL and continue to a bridge. Keep heading uphill with the river on the left. Soon afterwards, pass a 19th century ice house on the left.

2 3.3km: The path fords the river and climbs more steeply.

3 3.9km: Arrive at a saddle bisected by the MW (583m): TL and walk uphill (SE) alongside the MW.

18 4.8km: TR after the turret on the summit of **Slieve Donard (849m)** and descend S alongside the MW. From the **Bog of Donard**, head SE (away from the MW) and soon pick up a path.

10 7.2km: **See Map 2**. From the summit of **Chimney Rock Mountain (656m)**, retrace your steps. **See Map 1**. Cross the stile at the **Bog of Donard**. Then TL and head S with the MW on your left. This section can be boggy but walking on the MW is against the rules of the DRR.

19 9.6km: **See Map 2**. Where the MW angles to the left, bear right and head SW up the grassy slopes. Soon bear left and head S directly towards the summit of Rocky Mountain. From the summit of **Rocky Mountain (525m)**, retrace your steps to the **Bog of Donard**. **See Map 1**. Then TL onto the **Brandy Pad**.

4 13.5km: TL at a large cairn, heading SW up the slope on a rocky path. Keep SH across the summit of **Slieve Beg (596m)**. Shortly afterwards, pass a precipitous gully known as the **Devil's Coachroad**: take care. The path bends right (W) and descends towards a stream bed. Cross the stream bed and climb a steep path to the left of a line of boulders. Eventually, the line of boulders enters a broad rock garden: follow the faint path through the rocks directly up the slope. Cross the broad, flat summit of **Cove Mountain (655m)**. Soon head SW to a broad saddle, making sure that you avoid the dangerous cliffs to the E. From the saddle, climb S on a rocky path. If you lose the path, keep heading S straight up the slope. Finally, the path bends to the SW.

5 16.2km: At the summit of **Slievelamagan (704m)**, head SW on a faint path which soon disappears. Keep descending steeply SW, working your way in and out of rocks, towards a saddle above Ben Crom Reservoir. There is no easy way down this slope and it is slippery in the wet.

6 17.3km: **See Map 2**. At the **saddle**, keep SH and climb the slopes of Slieve Binnian on a rocky path. It is steep in places and you will need to clamber over a few rocks. Towards the top, the path becomes hard to follow. Pass just to the W of the large outcrops of the **North Tor (678m)**. Then, follow the path along the crest of the ridge. Approaching the next set of outcrops, the path forks: TR and climb directly towards the outcrops. Head around the left side of the first outcrop. A few minutes later, pass through a gap in a dry-stone wall. Immediately afterwards, TR on a path heading all the way around the right side of another outcrop. Immediately after the outcrop, head back up onto the crest of the ridge: ignore the faint path running SW and head S along the crest.

3 19.8km: Climb through a grassy cleft to arrive at the first summit of **Slieve Binnian (747m)**. Follow the path S down to a little saddle a few metres away.

Head downhill to the W on a faint path towards the Silent Valley Reservoir. After a few metres, ignore another faint path on the left, which heads (underneath some crags) towards a section of the MW. Instead, continue downhill towards the reservoir. After a minute or so, leave the path and head SW down the grassy slope for a few metres until you pick up another faint path. TL and head towards the base of some boulders to the S. The path passes below some small sections of the MW and afterwards, becomes faint. Clamber down some large boulders: you will now be heading towards Wee Binnian, the rocky peak below to the SW. After a few more minutes, the MW comes into view again and the path brings you towards it. A few metres from the MW, the path descends steeply over shale, roughly parallel to the wall. Climb over the MW where it re-emerges at a rock slab. Take care here: there are some metal rods, driven into the slab on the other side of the wall, which may help you to scramble down carefully. Now simply follow the wall steeply downhill. At a saddle, cross a stile. Then climb, still alongside the MW.

4 20.8km: When the MW disappears into some rock slabs, climb the last few metres to the summit of **Wee Binnian (460m)**. Head S for a few metres, then SW down through a steep cleft in the rocks. At a small grassy plateau, TR and head N alongside the rocks of the summit, which is just above on the right. Pass through a narrow gap in the rocks and then descend NW for a few metres to pick up a path. TL and follow it, initially SW. The path bends to the left until it heads directly towards the MW again. When you reach the MW, follow it downhill. Cross a saddle and then climb. When the MW bisects another dry-stone wall, pass through a gap in the other wall and continue following the MW, initially W.

5 21.4km: Arrive at the large boulder marking the summit of **Moolieve (332m)**. Continue following the MW, now to the SW. At a stile, cross the MW and continue descending alongside it. At the bottom of the slope, climb another stile: then head W to the access road for **Silent Valley Mountain Park**.

## Stage 2

From the access road, head N to the SE tip of the **Silent Valley Reservoir**. TL and walk along the top of the dam at the foot of the reservoir. At the SW corner of the reservoir, TR on a path along the edge of the water. Soon, the path moves away from the reservoir and starts to climb. A few metres afterwards, TR at a junction onto another path and continue climbing. Climb a stile and continue upwards on the path. The path makes a sharp left turn and then climbs to another stile: do not cross it but TR to walk alongside a fence for a few metres until you reach the MW again. Follow the MW upwards: this section can be boggy.

6 24.7km: **See Map 4**. When the MW makes a sharp turn to the right, keep following it. Pass through a gap in another wall and continue steeply uphill alongside the MW. The path here is faint and intermittent and this is a tough climb: at times you will need to clamber over rocks.

7 25.5km: **See Map 2.** Pass a stile and immediately afterwards, when the MW turns sharply left, TL and follow a faint path to the summit cairn of **Slievenaglogh (445m)**. Retrace your steps back to the stile, cross over and follow the MW to the NW: there is a faint path near the wall through the heather. After a level section, descend steeply over rocks. When the route levels again, the ground is boggy.

8 26.5km: **See Map 4.** TR, cross a stile and climb on a track known as '**Banns Road**'. **See Map 3.** Arrive at **Lough Shannagh (408m)**: TL off the main path to reach the shore of the lough. From there, TR and follow a small path which heads along the E side of the lough. Pass a stone shelter at the NE tip of the lough. Shortly afterwards, TR at a weir and proceed alongside a stream which narrows after a few minutes. Cross the stream on stones as soon as it is safe to do so. After crossing, TL and head back to the weir. Then TR and continue on the grassy path along the edge of the lough. When the path disappears, continue SH (ENE) straight up the hillside towards a ridge: the terrain is wet and boggy but you may find a faint path in places. On the ridge, TR and climb on a clear path. When

the path splits, in front of a rocky outcrop, take either path.

15 30.5km: From the summit of **Doan (594m)**, retrace your steps NW. From a sandy plateau, TR and head NE. At the **Ben Crom River**, bear right, heading SE. You should find a path: initially, you can cross to and fro over various little tributaries of the river as there are rough paths on either side. For now, you can use both sides of the river to your advantage, crossing over when it is preferable. However, soon the path on the W side of the river becomes better-defined and it makes more sense to use it.

9 31.9km: Cross the river and climb E: you may find a faint path. When the ground levels, bear right and head SE across rough grass and peat hags, keeping to the high ground: it is often boggy. Keep SE and start to climb: you may find a faint path. Arrive on the summit of **Ben Crom (526m)**. Retrace your steps to 9. From there, climb NW along the W side of the river to 16. Then head W across rough ground (no path) to 13: TL onto a path. TL at 12 and climb alongside the MW.

10 36.7km: **See Map 6.** TR at the summit of **Carn Mountain (588m)**. Follow the MW which heads W: ignore another wall heading S.

9 38.1km: Cross a stile and then keep SH to the trig point on the summit of **Slieve Muck (674m)**. Then descend steeply W alongside a wall. Cross a stile and Moyad Road.

## Stage 3

From Moyad Road, head W to another stile. Climb it and follow a wall uphill to the W.

14 40.2km: TL at the cairn on the summit of **Pigeon Rock Mountain (534m)** and continue alongside the wall. When the wall turns right, keep following it (downhill to the SW). Keep SH at a saddle and climb steeply SW, still beside the wall. Towards the top of the slope, bear right (leaving the wall) and head NW across open ground.

2 42.0km: From the summit of **Slievemoughanmore (559m)**, descend E. Do not be tempted to descend N as there are steep crags. Soon, descend steeply amongst rocks. Just before a grassy plateau, TL and contour around the slopes to the NW. Then descend NW across thick heather towards the right side of the saddle between Slievemoughanmore and Wee Slievemoughan. Keep NW along the right side of the saddle, staying below its highest point: there are peat hags to the left.

1 43.1km: From the pancake rocks on the summit of **Wee Slievemoughan (428m)**, descend S, aiming for the gap between Slievemoughanmore and Eagle Mountain. Work your way across the uneven terrain through peat hags.

13 44.2km: At the **Windy Gap (407m)**, climb a stile over a wall. Immediately afterwards, TR and climb steeply SW, now on the S side of the wall. Continue following the wall when it bends sharply to the left. Then, when it bends to the right, keep SH (SE) for a few metres to reach the summit cairn of **Eagle Mountain (638m)**. Return to the wall: TL, following it SW down to a saddle and then up the other side.

12 45.6km: **See Map 5.** When the wall bends right, head S and shortly, reach the summit cairn on **Shanlieve (626m)**. Head S on a faint path across open ground towards the broad summit of Finlieve. After 10min, the path disappears and you enter possibly the most challenging section of peat hags in the Mournes. In our opinion, it is wise not to drift too far to the W where the peat hags seem higher: stay fairly close to the E side of the plain where there are a few trees and the peat hags seem less intimidating. However, take care not to drift too far to the E as you will lose height.

3 48.0km: From the summit of **Finlieve (578m)**, descend SW on a faint path: ignore the path heading SE. When the path disappears, continue downhill across rough ground, aiming for the corner of a forest 2. As you approach the forest,

the ground is boggy.

2 49.9km: Just before the forest, cross two streams. Then pick up a faint path climbing SW up a grassy slope: the path is a short distance to the left of a wall and may be hard to spot in summer when the grass is long. When the path splits (easy to miss), keep SH (SW) on the fainter branch. At the end of the forest, head SW diagonally up a grassy slope (no path). TL on a grassy path just below a radio mast and continue climbing. Immediately after the mast, TR on a grassy path. Shortly, TL at a junction and descend towards a stile near a saddle. Cross the stile: then TL and climb.

3 53.2km: From the summit of **Slievemeen (472m)**, retrace your steps back to the saddle. Then keep SH and climb.

4 54.0km: Reach the trig point on the summit of **Slievemartin (485m)**.

## Stage 4

From the trig point, head towards the radio mast. A few minutes later, cross a stile. Immediately afterwards, TL on a grassy path alongside an old wall. Shortly afterwards, bear right on a path, leaving the wall: descend N towards a gap in trees (below the broad summit of Crenville). The path soon heads E of the gap: you will need to TL (leaving the path) and aim towards the gap. The ground is boggy and uneven (with long grass in summer).

5 54.9km: At the gap, cross a fence. Then climb NE along the right side of the gap: at times there is a faint path through the challenging terrain. Soon follow the line of a fence. After a while, TL and climb through grassy tussocks towards the trees on the summit. From the post on the summit of **Crenville (460m)**, head NW (passing just to the right of trees). Descend NW to a post at the edge of Rostrevor Forest (**IG J204189**). The next section is very difficult both in terms of terrain and navigation: you will need to head W through the thick forest for 200m to the junction at 6 (**IG J202189**). Getting into the forest is the trickiest part because the branches at the edges are overgrown: once inside, it is marginally easier but there is no path or clear channel to follow.

**Warning**: if you emerge onto a narrow path or a board-walk, running NE/SW, this is a mountain-biking track and you should not walk on it. To do so would place yourself and the bikers at great risk of injury or death. Retreat back into the forest and work your way SW parallel to the biking track. The junction you are looking for should only be a short distance away.

6 56.0km: TR at a junction and descend on a track. After a while, TR onto another track.

7 57.6km: TL onto another track. Shortly afterwards, TR and go through a gate. The main path here is a mountain-biking track and you should not walk along it: keep SH after the gate and climb on a grassy path. Shortly afterwards, cross the biking track and keep SH, climbing on a faint grassy path heading up towards the next summit. After a difficult climb across heather, reach the summit of **Slievemeel (420m)**. Descend N towards a lake. When the lake slips out of sight, aim for a narrow gap which heads into the forest from the junction of two fences.

8 59.0km: At the gap, continue N on a faint path alongside a fence. You may have to push through branches which encroach on the path. When a tree blocks your way, cross to the other side of the fence; shortly afterwards, cross back. Soon, TR onto a broad path through **Kilbroney Red Bog**. Shortly after crossing a bridge, turn sharp right on a broad path. A few minutes later, TL on a grassy path. TR at a junction. Go through a gap in a fence. Then bear left, climbing across grassy slopes: ignore the path running SH uphill from the gap.

9 61.5km: **See Map 6**. From the summit of **Tievedockaragh (473m)**, head N. Shortly afterwards TR and walk alongside a wall and then a fence. Just before another section of wall, TL and cross the fence: pick up a path.

10 62.9km: TL onto an old bog road. At the end of it, TR onto a broad path heading initially SE. Soon the path bends around to the left and makes its way N directly towards Pierces Castle. Ignore any offshoots on the right.

10 63.5km: Finally, the path climbs up through boulders to arrive on the summit of **Pierces Castle (467m)**. Proceed to the left of the enormous boulder on the summit and pick up a path heading down to the N. Shortly afterwards, descend a steep rock step. Just afterwards, the path descends to the NE, slightly to the right of the ridge: but soon it arrives on top of the broad ridge again. Keep heading N. The path becomes faint in places: keep near the crest of the ridge. When the path descends to a small saddle, keep SH (N) and head up the slope on the other side of the saddle to arrive on a long, broad plateau. Keep N along the plateau to reach the summit of **Tornamrock (390m)** 9. Keep to the left of the rocky outcrops and descend directly towards Rocky Mountain (NW): the path is faint in places. Keep SH across the saddle between Tornamrock and Rocky Mountain and climb on a faint path.

8 65.6km: From the summit cairn of **Rocky Mountain (405m)**, descend NE across open ground towards **Rocky River**. Ford the river on boulders (which can be slippery): the riverbank is steep in places so you may have to walk along the banks to find a safe place to cross. Then head NE to the saddle between Cock Mountain and Hen Mountain: from there, TR and climb directly up the slopes of Cock Mountain.

6 68.4km: From the NE summit of **Cock Mountain (505m)**, descend NE to a saddle. Then climb NE to the summit of **Slievenamiskan (444m)** 5. Descend E towards the W side of a dam wall: make sure that you pass S of the rocks just W of the dam. Descend alongside the dam. Cross a bridge over the dam run-off canals and then pass through a gate. Note that, although this is a popular route, it is not clear whether walkers are actually permitted here. Head along a lane and climb a metal gate. TR and walk up the Kilkeel Road (B27). Reach **Spelga Reservoir car park**.

## Stage 5

From the car park, head briefly E up the road to a gate by a stream. Go through the gate and TL, fording a stream. Head NW up the grassy slopes.

4 71.3km: From the summit of **Spelga (472m)**, head NE along the ridge. The ground is boggy: for much of the way there is a faint grassy path. Reach a small rocky cairn on the summit of **Spaltha (479m)** where the path forks: take the right branch. Soon, look for a fence to the NE.

7 72.5km: A few hundred metres before the fence, TR on a faint, grassy path (easy to miss) which descends into a shallow valley (filled with peat hags). Keep SH when the path disappears at a particularly boggy section. Afterwards, pick up a faint path which soon runs SW along the top of an old bog road. Just before the path starts its final descent to Spelga Reservoir, TL on a path and climb. When you meet a broad grassy path, TL and climb towards the summit of Slievenamuck.

2 74.7km: Keep SH across the summit of **Slievenamuck (504m)** on a clear path. Shortly afterwards, TR on another path and descend.

1 75.3km: Cross a stile and reach **Ott Mountain car park**. TL and walk down the road (NE) for a few metres. Then, cross the road and pick up a stony path heading SE. After a few minutes, TR at a junction of tracks. Shortly afterwards, bear right and leave the path: climb S up a ridge to the summit of **Ott Mountain (524m;** 12). Descend SE and then climb E towards the MW. TL and head NE along the MW.

11 77.6km: **See Map 3**. From the summit of **Slieve Loughshannagh (619m)**, descend to a **saddle (511m)**. Then climb again, still following the MW.

12 78.6km: From the summit of **Slieve Meelbeg (708m)**, descend to another

saddle and then climb up the other side. When the MW bisects another dry-stone wall, keep heading uphill (NE).

13 79.6km: Pass the summit cairn of **Slieve Meelmore (687m)**. Shortly afterwards, TR and cross a stile at a stone turret built into a corner of the MW. Follow the MW SE downhill. Towards the bottom of the slope, the rocks are steep. At a saddle, start climbing, initially alongside the MW. Soon, the path drifts right up across the slope and then splits into a number of paths. Take the path furthest to the left (the steepest one) and climb. Now there is a confusing array of different paths: work your way upwards, soon heading back towards the MW again. Arrive back at the MW, just above the point at which it re-emerges at the top of some steep crags. Now climb alongside the MW, working your way up through rocks. Just before the summit, pick up a clear path.

14 80.7km: From the corner of the MW just NW of the summit of **Slieve Bearnagh (739m)**, follow the MW downhill to the NE. After a few minutes, bear right around some boulders and then follow a path E around the base of the **North Tor of Slieve Bearnagh**. There are a number of paths here: use the widest one, which is roughly in the middle. The path circles around the North Tor to arrive back at the MW again. Follow the MW steeply downhill. Eventually, the path levels out and skirts to the right of a group of rocks. Afterwards, the path continues to drift away from the MW. When you reach another path, TL and descend steeply on some rock steps.

15 81.8km: **See Map 1**. Keep SH (NE) past the large cairn at the **Hares' Gap (437m)**. Then climb steeply alongside the MW, to the right of a rocky outcrop.

16 82.6km: From the summit cairn on **Slievenaglogh (586m)**, keep following the MW as it undulates along the ridge. Pass over the indistinct summit of **Slieve Corragh (641m)**. Descend briefly and then climb steeply. Cross a stile beside the turret near the summit of Slieve Commedagh and walk NE.

17 84.8km: After a few minutes, arrive at the summit cairn of **Slieve Commedagh (765m)**. Retrace your steps back to the MW: TL and descend SE alongside the MW. From, the saddle at 3, TL and retrace your steps.

S/F 2 90.0km: Finish at the main entrance to **Donard Park car park**.

*The view of Hen Mountain from Pierces Castle*

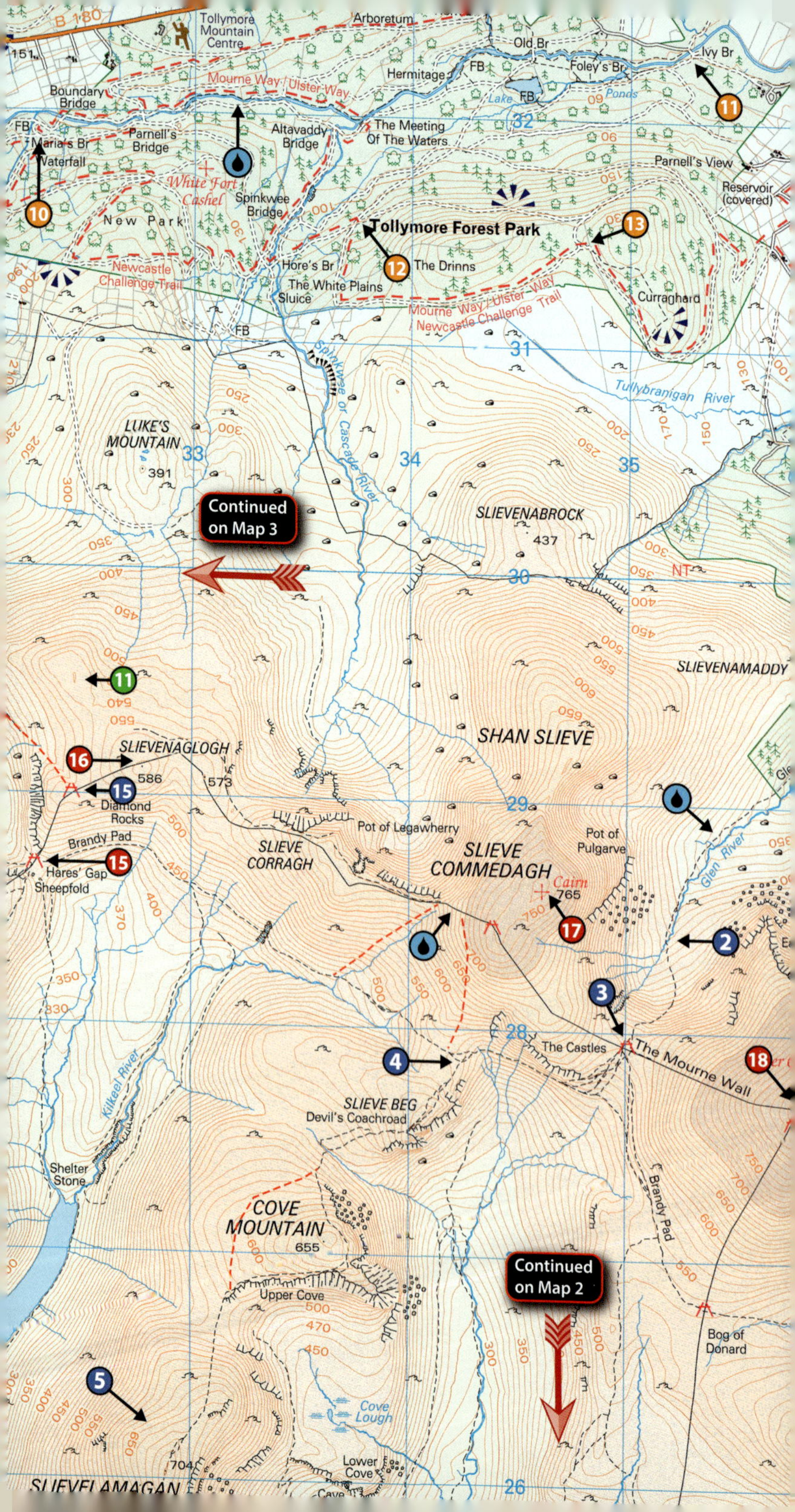

Tollymore Mountain Centre
Arboretum
Old Br
Ivy Br
Foley's Br
Hermitage
Lake
Ponds
Boundary Bridge
Mourne Way/Ulster Way
Maria's Br
Waterfall
Parnell's Bridge
Altavaddy Bridge
The Meeting Of The Waters
Parnell's View
Reservoir (covered)
White Fort Cashel
Spinkwee Bridge
New Park
Tollymore Forest Park
The Drinns
Newcastle Challenge Trail
Hore's Br
The White Plains
Sluice
Curraghard
Mourne Way/Ulster Way Newcastle Challenge Trail
Tullybranigan River
Spinkwee or Cascade River
LUKE'S MOUNTAIN
391
SLIEVENABROCK
437
Continued on Map 3
SLIEVENAMADDY
SHAN SLIEVE
SLIEVENAGLOGH
586
573
Diamond Rocks
Brandy Pad
Hares' Gap
Sheepfold
Pot of Legawherry
SLIEVE CORRAGH
SLIEVE COMMEDAGH
Pot of Pulgarve
Cairn
765
Glen River
The Castles
The Mourne Wall
Kilkeel River
SLIEVE BEG
Devil's Coachroad
Shelter Stone
COVE MOUNTAIN
655
Brandy Pad
Upper Cove
Continued on Map 2
Bog of Donard
Cove Lough
Lower Cove
704
SLIEVELAMAGAN

Map 1
NEWCASTLE
S/F 8
S/F 2
S/F 5
Lecale Way / Ulster Way
Mourne Golf Club
Slieve Donard Hotel
GAA Ground
St Cillian Fort
Earthwork
Shimna or Tollymore River
Shimna House
Tipperary Wood
Tipperary Lane
B 180
Islands Park
Weir
Newcastle Centre
Swimming Pool (Outdoor)
Hotel
Donard Park
Black Rock
Rock Swimming Pool (Outdoor)
Greenhill (YMCA Centre)
DRINNAHILLY
Waterfalls
Donard Bridge
Waterfall
Craignagore
Police Station
Newcastle Yacht Club
Harbour
Lifeboat Station
South Promenade
Donard Forest
Ice House
Lindsay's Leap
Granite Trail
Black Stairs
Quarry
THOMAS'S MOUNTAIN
Drinneevar
Kilkeel Road
Donard Cove
MILLSTONE MOUNTAIN
Sheepfold
Srupatrick
Maggy's Leap
Armor's Hole
Leganabruchan
Shannagh-More Outdoor Education Centre
The Broad Cove
Shannagh-More
Carn
Trig Pillar
Living Rock
E DONARD
CROSSONE
Glen Fofanny
Glen Fofanny River
Rookahill
Raven Rocks
Bloody Bridge
Bloody Bridge River
St Mary's Stream
St Mary's Church
Crannoge
Quarry Track
Reservoir
Mineral Railway (disused)
Dulusk Cove
Carr's Face
SLIEVENAGARRAGH
William's Harbour
38
39
0
1km

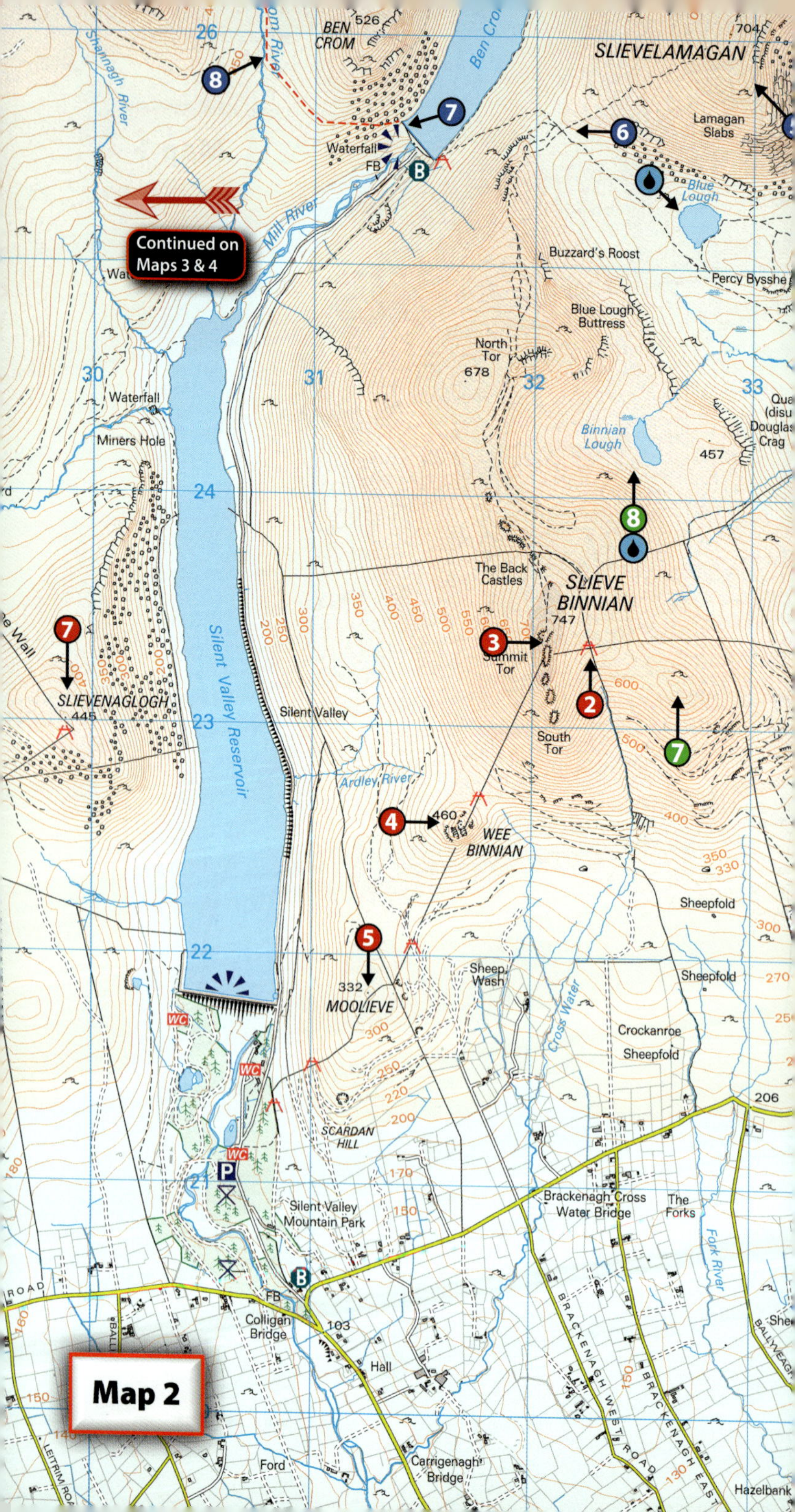
BEN CROM
526
Ben Crom
SLIEVELAMAGAN
704
Lamagan Slabs
Shannagh River
Waterfall
FB
Mill River
Continued on Maps 3 & 4
Blue Lough
Buzzard's Roost
Percy Bysshe
Blue Lough Buttress
North Tor
678
Binnian Lough
457
Douglas Crag
Waterfall
Miners Hole
Silent Valley Reservoir
The Back Castles
SLIEVE BINNIAN
747
Summit Tor
South Tor
SLIEVENAGLOGH
445
Silent Valley
Ardley River
460
WEE BINNIAN
Sheepfold
332
MOOLIEVE
Sheep Wash
Cross Water
Crockanroe Sheepfold
SCARDAN HILL
206
Silent Valley Mountain Park
Brackenagh Cross Water Bridge
The Forks
Fork River
Colligan Bridge
103
Hall
BRACKENAGH WEST ROAD
BRACKENAGH EAST
Carrigenagh Bridge
Ford
Hazelbank
LEITRIM ROAD
Map 2

CHIMNEY ROCK MOUNTAIN
656
10
BLAEBERRY MOUNTAIN
19
ROCKY MOUNTAIN
525
Continued on Map 1
SPENCES MOUNTAIN
517
9
Lower Cove
Cave
Annalong Wood
Weir
Annalong River
LONG SEEFIN
20
21
Dunnywater
Sluice
FB
Mourne Wall
ROUND SEEFIN
217
CARRICK DIG
1
Sheepfold
CARRICK LITTLE
S/F 1
Dunnywater Bridge
O'Rourke's Park
153
91
QUARTER ROAD
Glasdromain GAA
MILL ROAD
OLDTOWN ROAD
OLDTOWN LANE
SABBATH HILL
BALLYVEAGHMORE ROAD
The Long Stone
Longstone GAA
Longstone Park
MAJORS HILL
MONEYDARRAGH
1km
Spences River
Playing

Map 3
0
1km
Tullybrack
FB
DRUMBONIFF ROAD
OFANNY SCHOOL ROAD
MILL ROAD
FB
Ford
Sheepfold
229
Rath
GHILL ROAD
BRYANSFORD ROAD
203
31
26
27
28
FOFANNY ROAD
169
Ford
Knockvegrana
Water
Works
Sheepfold
Coolnamah
Sluice
30
Sheepfold
Sheepfold
Sheepfold
Ardglash
Sheepfold
CRAIGDOO
407
Sheepfold
296
KINNAHALLA
KINNAHALLA ROAD
Sheepfold
Lugagour
287
Water
Treatment
Works
Fish
Pass
Weir
FB
SLIEVENAMAN ROAD
29
Fofanny
Sheepfolds
Glenaveagh Stream
SPALTHA
479
BUTTER
MOUNTAIN
FB
Glenaveagh
Bridge
S/F
4
SPELGA
472
SLIEVENAMUCK
Spelga Pass
B27
River Bann
FB
315
WC
Sheepfold
Ford
Weir
FB
SLIEVENAMISKAN
444
OTT
MOUNTAIN
Spelga Dam
(Reservoir)
557
Continued
on Map 6
Continued
on Map 4
588
Deers
Meadow
River
Bann
Source of
River Bann
Sheep

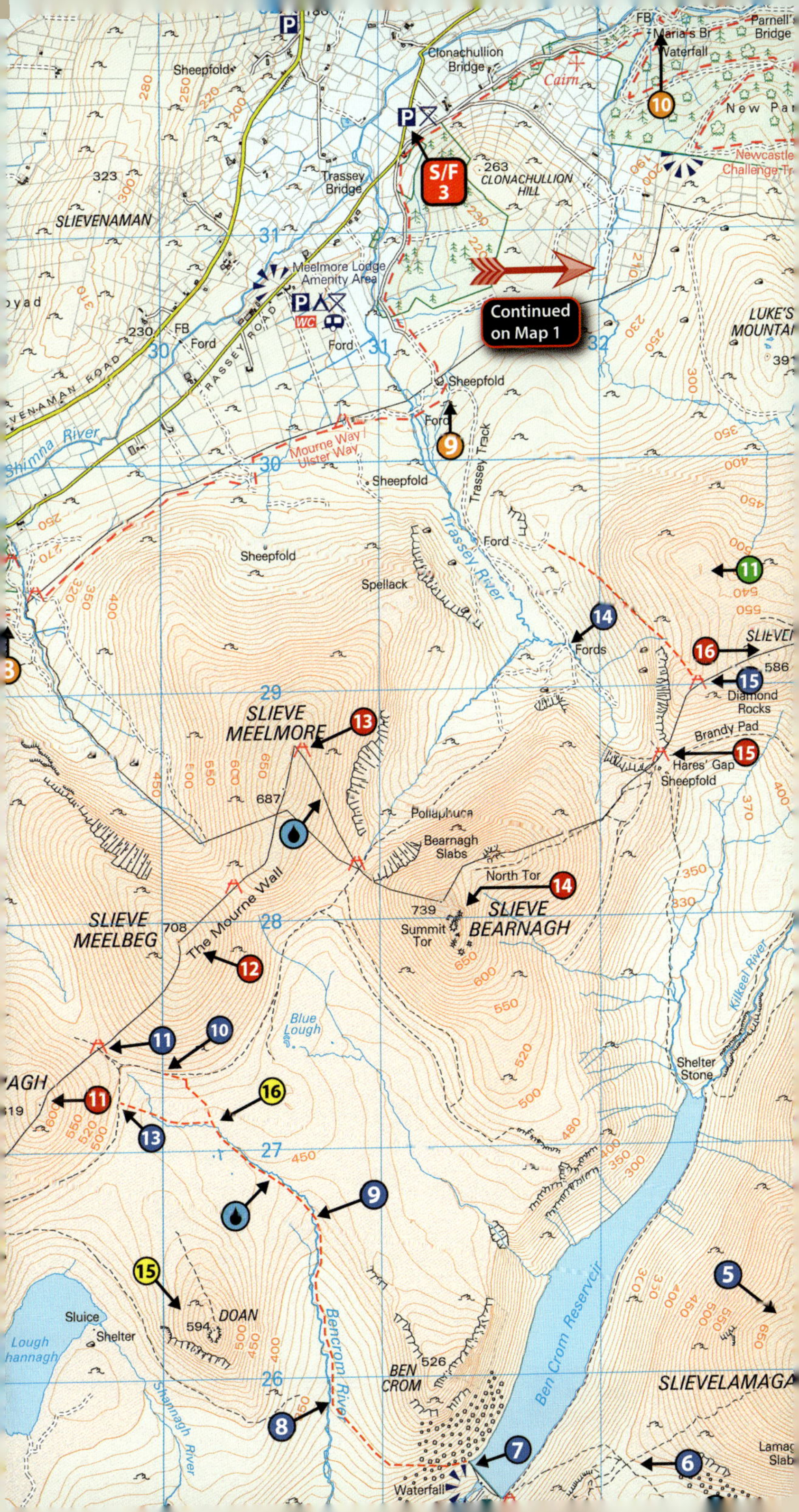

Sheepfold
Clonachullion Bridge
Cairn
Maria's Br
Waterfall
Parnell's Bridge
New Par
S/F 3
263
CLONACHULLION HILL
Newcastle Challenge Tr
323
Trassey Bridge
SLIEVENAMAN
Meelmore Lodge Amenity Area
WC
Continued on Map 1
LUKE'S MOUNTAI
FB
Ford
TRASSEY ROAD
SLIEVENAMAN ROAD
Sheepfold
Shimna River
Mourne Way / Ulster Way
Trassey Track
Trassey River
Spellack
Fords
SLIEVE
586
Diamond Rocks
Brandy Pad
Hares' Gap
Sheepfold
SLIEVE MEELMORE
687
Pollaphuca
Bearnagh Slabs
North Tor
739
Summit Tor
SLIEVE BEARNAGH
SLIEVE MEELBEG
708
The Mourne Wall
Blue Lough
Kilkeel River
Shelter Stone
AGH
DOAN
594
Sluice
Shelter
Lough hannagh
Bencrom River
BEN CROM
526
Ben Crom Reservoir
Shannagh River
SLIEVELAMAGA
Lamag Slab
Waterfall

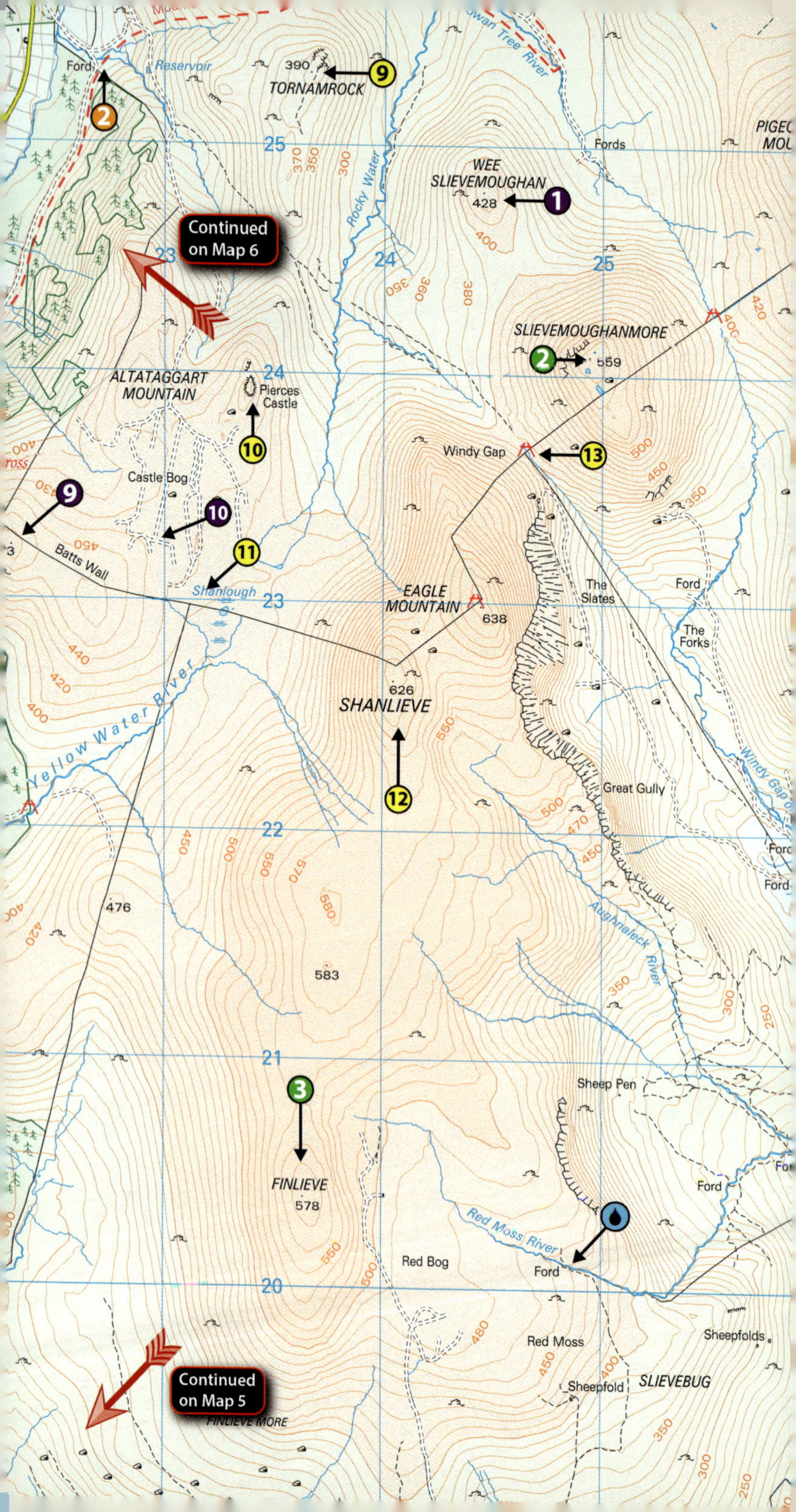

Ford
Reservoir
390
TORNAMROCK
Rocky Water
WEE SLIEVEMOUGHAN
428
Fords
Continued on Map 6
SLIEVEMOUGHANMORE
559
ALTATAGGART MOUNTAIN
Pierces Castle
Windy Gap
Castle Bog
Batts Wall
Shanlough
EAGLE MOUNTAIN
638
626
SHANLIEVE
The Slates
Ford
The Forks
Yellow Water River
Great Gully
Windy Gap
Aughnaleck River
476
583
Sheep Pen
FINLIEVE
578
Ford
Red Moss River
Red Bog
Ford
Red Moss
Sheepfolds
Sheepfold
SLIEVEBUG
Continued on Map 5
FINLIEVE MORE

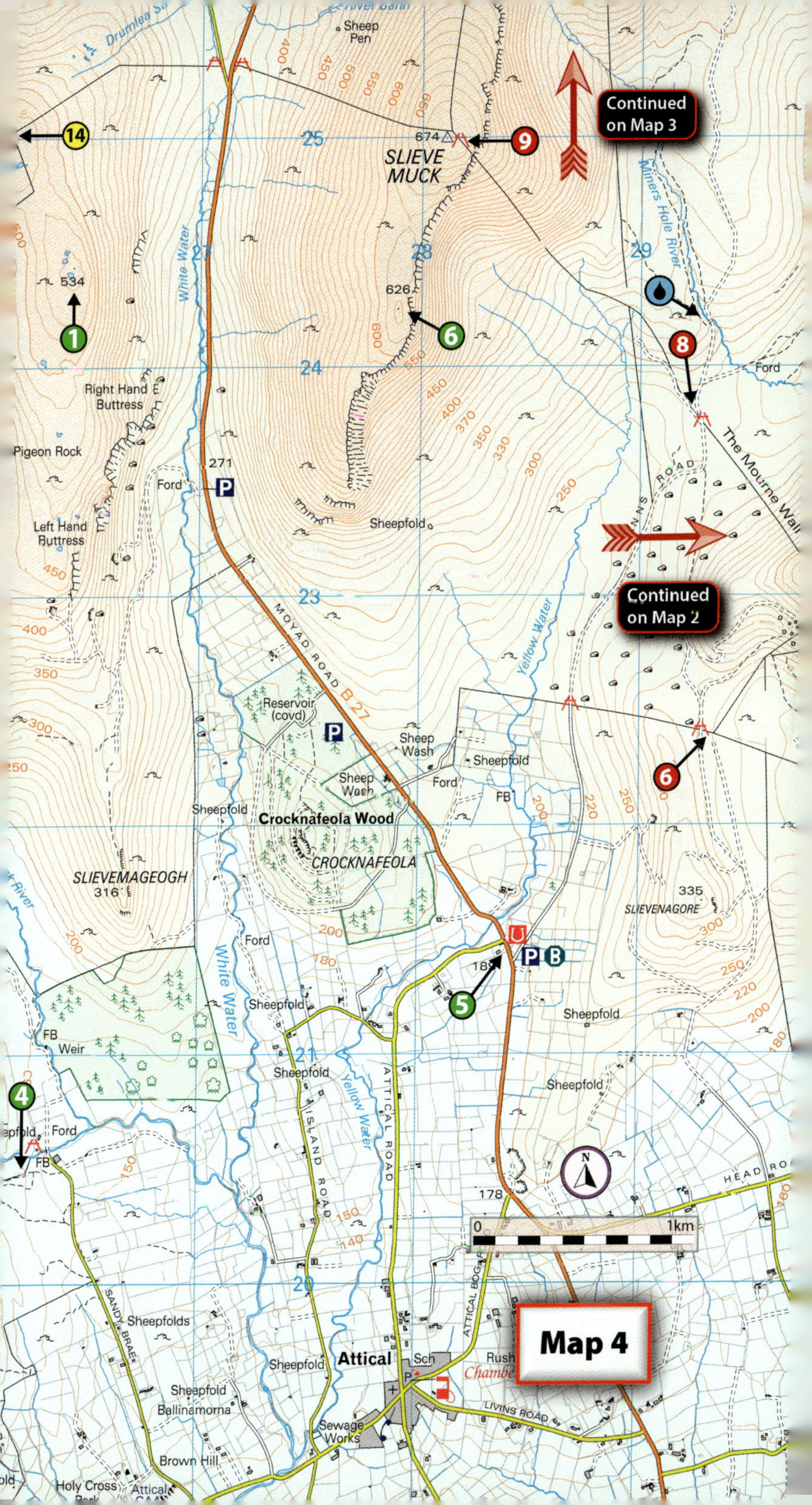
Continued on Map 3
Continued on Map 2
Map 4
SLIEVE MUCK
674
626
534
Right Hand Buttress
Pigeon Rock
Left Hand Buttress
Ford
271
Sheepfold
The Mourne Wall
Miners Hole River
White Water
Yellow Water
MOYAD ROAD B27
Reservoir (covd)
Sheep Wash
Sheepfold
Crocknafeola Wood
CROCKNAFEOLA
SLIEVEMAGEOGH
316
SLIEVENAGORE
335
FB
Weir
Ford
ISLAND ROAD
ATTICAL ROAD
ATTICAL BOG
HEAD ROAD
LIVINS ROAD
SANDY BRAE
Sheepfolds
Attical
Sch
Rush
Sewage Works
Ballinamorna
Brown Hill
Holy Cross
0
1km
178

Map 5
Continued on Map 6
SLIEVE ROOSLEY
LOWER KNOCKBARRAGH
Yellow Water Picnic Area
Weir
FB
Ford
172
LECKAN MORE
355
Kilbroney Red Bog
KILBRONEY ROAD
NEWTOWN ROAD
Monastry
Sheepfold
126
Carnacloosha Stream
Sheep Pen
Wash
LECKAN BEG
232
Kilbroney River
SLIEVEMEEL
420
Ford
113
Industrial Estate
Reservoir (covd)
97
Rostrevor Forest
Sheepfold
THUNDERS HILL
Kilbroney House
Ch (in ruins)
St Bronagh's Well
Cemetery
Standing Stone
Rath
Weir
The Fallow
Sheepfold
44
SLIEVEDERMOT
CRENVILLE
460
Cemy
Weir
Rostrevor River
Fairy Glen
Playing Field
Kilbroney Park
WC
CLOUGHMORE RD
SLIEVEBANE
SHORE RD
S/F 7
Glen Stream
SLIEVEMARTIN
485
Cairn
Garage
Rostrevor Oakwood
Cloghmore
Cloghmore Glen
National Nature Reserve
Rostrevor Quay
SHORE ROAD
Fiddlers Green
SLIEVEMEEN
472
SLIEVEFADDA
The Clasha
Ballynagelty

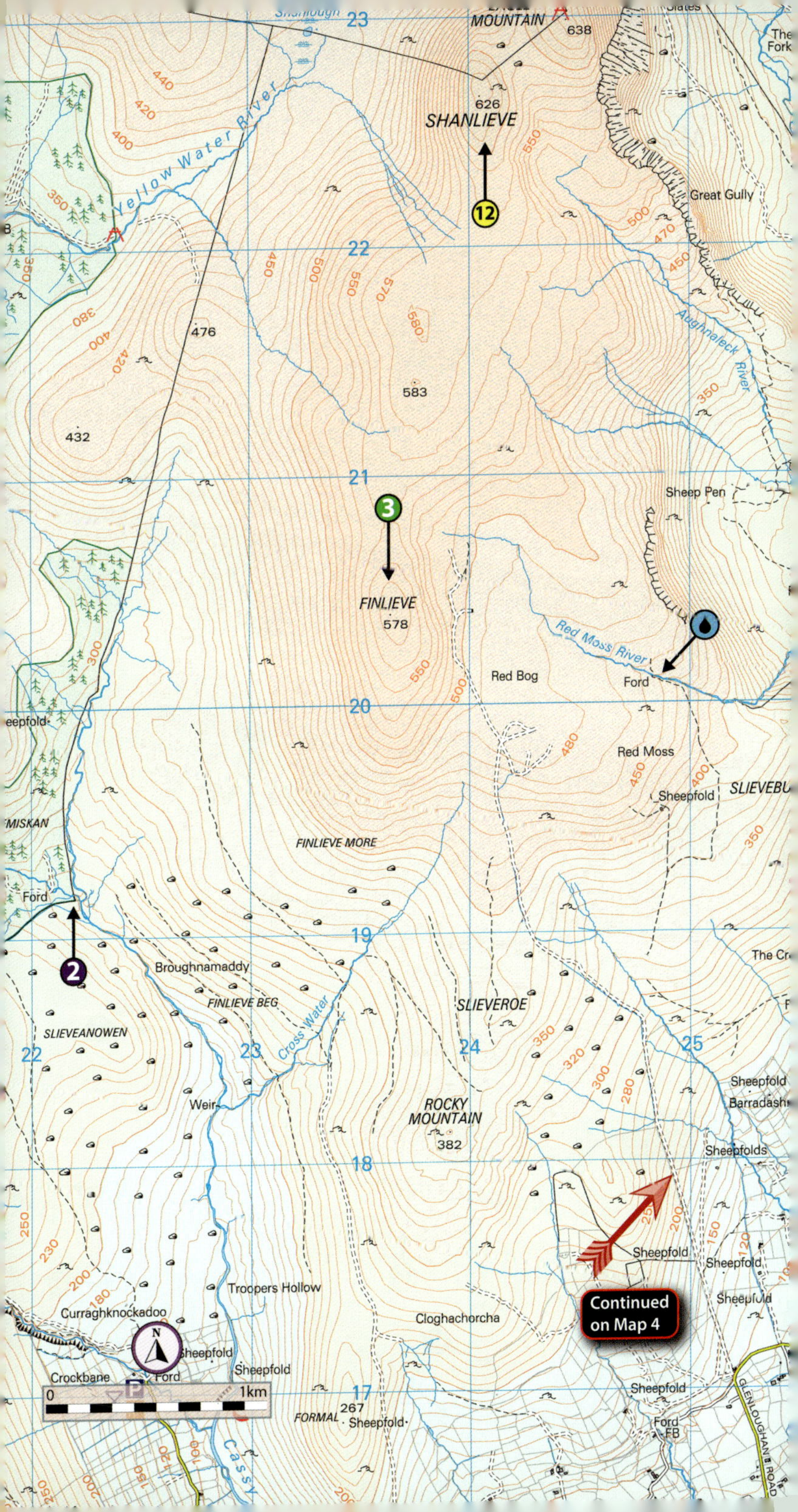

MOUNTAIN
638
626
SHANLIEVE
Yellow Water River
Great Gully
Aughnaleck River
476
583
432
Sheep Pen
FINLIEVE
578
Red Moss River
Red Bog
Ford
Red Moss
Sheepfold
FINLIEVE MORE
Ford
Broughnamaddy
FINLIEVE BEG
SLIEVEANOWEN
Cross Water
SLIEVEROE
Weir
ROCKY MOUNTAIN
382
Sheepfold
Barradash
Sheepfolds
Sheepfold
Sheepfold
Sheepfold
Troopers Hollow
Curraghknockadoo
Cloghachorcha
Continued on Map 4
Sheepfold
Sheepfold
Crockbane
Ford
0
1km
267
FORMAL
Sheepfold
Sheepfold
Ford
FB
GLENLOUGHAN ROAD

Map 6
S/F 6
Continued on Map 5
Motte
Cashel
Raths
Ford
New Bridge
KILKEEL ROAD
Sheepfold Ford
NEW LINE ROAD
LEITRIM HILL
LEITRIM ROAD
SANDBANK ROAD
Rockyriver Bridge
Sheepfolds
HEN MOUNTAIN
West Tor
Summit Tor
The Tower
South Tor
Rocky River
SHEEP HILL
Leitrim
Weir
Shankys River
Leitrim Lodge
ROCKY MOUNTAIN
Mourne Way / Ulster Way
Rowan Tree River
Reservoir
TORNAMROCK
Fords
WEE SLIEVEMOUGHAN
Rocky Water
SLIEVEMOUGHANMO
ALTATAGGART MOUNTAIN
Pierces Castle
Windy Gap
Cross
Castle Bog
TIEVEDOCKARAGH
Batts Wall
Shanlough
EAGLE MOUNTAIN
The Slates

Sheepfolds
SPALTHA
479
BUTTER MOUNTAIN
SLIEVENAMAN ROAD
Weir
FB
Fofanny Dam (Reservoir)
S/F 4
SPELGA
472
SLIEVENAMUCK
Spelga Pass
River Bann
B 27
SLIEVENAMISKAN
444
315
Sheepfold
Ford
Weir
Continued on Map 3
LOUGHS
OTT MOUNTAIN
Spelga Dam (Reservoir)
557
588
Deers Meadow
River Bann
Drumlea Stream
Source of River Bann
Sheep Pen
PIGEON ROCK MOUNTAIN
534
674
SLIEVE MUCK
626
White Water
Right Hand Buttress
Pigeon Rock
Left Hand Buttress
271
Ford
Sheepfold
Continued on Map 4
0
1km
MOYAD ROAD
Yellow Water